CODEPENDENCY CYCLE RECOVERY

Be Codependent No More and Recover Your Self-Esteem NOW, Cure Your Soul from Emotional Abuse - Stop Being Manipulated and Controlled by Narcissists and Sociopaths

By

DANIEL ANDERSON

PREFACE

© Copyright 2019 - All rights reserved.

The content contained within this book may not be reproduced, duplicated or transmitted without direct written permission from the author or the publisher.

Under no circumstances will any blame or legal responsibility be held against the publisher, or author, for any damages, reparation, or monetary loss due to the information contained within this book. Either directly or indirectly.

Legal Notice:

This book is copyright protected. This book is only for personal use. You cannot amend, distribute, sell, use, quote or paraphrase any part, or the content within this book, without the consent of the author or publisher.

Disclaimer Notice:

Please note the information contained within this document is for educational and entertainment purposes only. All effort has been executed to present accurate, up to date, and reliable, complete information. No warranties of any kind are declared or implied. Readers acknowledge that the author is not engaging in the rendering of legal, financial, medical or professional advice. The content within this book has been derived from various sources. Please consult a licensed professional before attempting any techniques outlined in this book.

By reading this document, the reader agrees that under no circumstances is the author responsible for any losses, direct or indirect, which are incurred as a result of the use of information contained within this document, including, but not limited to, — errors, omissions, or inaccuracies.

TABLE OF CONTENT

PREFACE 2
CHAPTER 1 UNDERSTANDING
CODEPENDENCY 7
   What Is Codependency? 7
   Understanding Codependency 12
   Codependency - Who Am I without
   Others? 18
   Codependency - Being Dependent on
   Other's Dependency 24
   Codependence in Your Life 27
   Codependence: The Flip Side to
   Narcissism 31
   Codependency and How It Affects
   Individuals 33
CHAPTER 2 CHARACTERISTICS AND
SYMPTOMS OF CODEPENDENT PEOPLE .. 35
   Are You Codependent? 35
   Pointers of Codependency 41
   Symptoms of Codependency 45
   3 Ways to Spot the Damaging Symptoms
   of Codependency 52
   Codependency - Identifying Its Causes
   and Effects 56
   Recognizing Codependent Behavior 62

CHAPTER 3 PROBLEMS AND RISKS ASSOCIATED WITH CODEPENDENTS AND THEIR RELATIONSHIPS 66

Codependency - A Crippling Relationship Problem 66
Codependency: Effect of Self-Esteem on Relationships 69
2 Biggest Codependent Traps You Might Be Falling Into 76
Codependence: A Manifestation of the Adult Child Syndrome 80
Narcissists are also Codependents 98

CHAPTER 4 START LOVING YOURSELF AND STOP BEING CODPENDENT 105

Do You Know Who You Are? 105
Steps to Understanding and Accepting Who You Are 109
Love Yourself for Your Own Sake 112
Accept Who You Are 115
Self Esteem - 5 Ways to Feel Better about Who You Are 118
Learning to Love Who You Are 122
Six Tips for Loving the Fabulous Person You Are 126
Six Pillars of Self Esteem - Accept Yourself for Who You Are 130
Loving Yourself for Who You Are 134
Discard Approval, Love and Accept Yourself 137

CHAPTER 5 HEALING AND RECOVERING FROM NARCISSISM AND EMOTIONAL ABUSE 141
   Discover Your Level of Narcissism............ 141
   Healing from A Relationship With A Narcissist 146
   Recovery from Narcissistic Abuse - To Get Your Life Back on Track....................... 150
   Emotional Abuse - 8 Steps to Recovery 153
   Best Tips to Recover from Narcissistic Abuse 158

CHAPTER 6 OVERCOMING AND RECOVERING FROM CODEPENDENCY ... 160
   Shedding Codependency - 3 Tips for Overcoming Codependent Tendencies 160
   Overcome Codependency - Discover the Freedom of Emotional Independence....... 163
   Three Ways to Overcome Codependent Relationships 169
   Recovering from Codependency 172
   Healing Codependency 177

CHAPTER 1

UNDERSTANDING CODEPENDENCY

What Is Codependency?

Codependence (or codependency) is usually defined as a behavior where an individual exhibits too much, and often inappropriate, caring for persons who depend on him or her. Another term associated with being "codependent" is enabling. In other words, being codependent is enabling the destructive behavior of an individual close to you to continue. It can also mean an individual may rely on the emotions and opinions of others around them to determine how they feel about themselves.

There are many things to consider before labeling yourself an enabler or codependent. No one should consider him or herself an enabler or codependent without first honestly reviewing their situation and environment. Being compassionate, sympathetic or empathetic to a suffering individual's predicament does not necessarily mean you are an enabler or a codependent. If you, by chance, are allowing an active alcoholic to live in your house free of charge while you pay the bills and this has gone on for a while now, well, you may be codependent. The reason being is you are enabling them to continue their destructive behaviors toward themselves and you. Taking little to none of the appropriate action to help a sick individual get well is a good sign of co-dependence.

One drawback many codependents experience is self-identification. If the destructive behavior has gone on for years, they may find themselves subconsciously sabotaging the sick individual's chances of getting better. A common fear is, "If they get better, what will happen to me? I won't be needed anymore." The disease of alcoholism and drug addiction is sometimes called a family disease because of all the people it affects. To some degree, everyone who lives with or is close to an active alcoholic or drug addict is sick. Years of destructive and sporadic behaviors of the alcoholic or drug addict will make a sick person out of anyone. Nearly no one is immune, employers, friends, coworkers, and especially the immediate family members.

Another situation for a codependent may be the result of being raised by an active alcoholic or drug addict. Usually what happens for the codependent in this scenario is they are overwhelming dependent on the actions, emotions, and opinions of others (such as a parent) to identify who they are. They are, in a sense, grown to believe they are incapable of living a successful life and usually suffer from extremely low self-esteem and possibly depression or other psychological disorders.

Codependent then implies that one is dependent psychologically on one who is dependent on a substance, behavior or another thing.

Codependents are those amongst us who worry obsessively about others. Most codependents were emotionally abused as children. They were made to feel psychologically invisible, and very often suffered various forms of abuse, including physical, sexual, verbal or psychological. The consistent theme amongst codependents is that they can think for others, but not for themselves.

Codependents pair off in relationships. It is not possible to have a codependent relationship with one who is not codependent. Noncodependents do not appreciate feeling smothered, overly relied upon for their partner's sense of satisfaction, and do not enjoy empty praise.

Codependents tend to whine and complain rather than act on their behalf. They complain about how sorry they feel for themselves and wallow on sounding as if they prefer the world see them as the martyrs they falsely believe that they are.

On a deep unconscious level, codependents are manipulators who are seeking a sense of validation from others. They manipulate others by their insatiable need to please others. In the pleasing of others, the codependent is in search of a return. The return is the notion that the object of their attention now 'owes' them. The object of the codependents attention is seen as a source of a much-needed sense of self.

Codependents do not cope well. Because they do not understand how to nurture their self, and because their childhood wounds are very deep, codependents are blind to the idea that their intentions are skewed and manipulative. Because in their minds they view themselves as being one who is giving, they are unable to see the error of their manipulative ways.

Codependents are flustered souls, who ultimately wind up feeling exasperated. Nothing that they thought might help them feel loved has worked. They have smothered others to the point of draining the ones that they loved, and wind up blaming others for their inability to love the codependent no matter how hard the codependent tries to love them.

One solution for someone who is suffering from codependency and would like to learn how to live without it is to attend some type of group support meetings. There, an individual can find freedom from the years of negative programming they experienced as a child, teenager or adult.

Understanding Codependency

The term codependency was originally coined by researchers studying the dynamics of alcohol addiction in families. It became clear to those who worked with alcoholics and their families that there was a very unhealthy two-way dependency created when a family member was addicted to alcohol.

Since then the term codependency has been expanded and used to describe almost any type of relationship where the dependent partner may be physically and psychologically dependent or addicted to a substance or may have chronic emotional, physical or financial problems.

The codependent partner tries to control the relationship. To keep the relationship from changing the codependent partner takes charge of the dependent partner by making excuses, hiding destructive behaviors, pitying him/her and generally enabling the dysfunctional pattern to continue.

A codependent person is someone who often shows excessive or even inappropriate caring for the dependent person. Both partners "need" each other in an unhealthy, symbiotic way.

Codependent people will often come from families where their personal needs were secondary to the needs of the family. The family may have been dealing with an addiction or some other difficult chronic problem. Codependents are somehow made to feel responsible for other family members who depend on them in an unhealthy way. They learn to repress their feelings and serve mainly to comfort and care for someone else.

As adults, codependent people are at greater risk to form relationships with others who are needy or emotionally unavailable. The familiar feeling of denying one's own emotions for the sake of someone else's is a strong pull towards repeating the early family dynamic.

Once they enter into a relationship codependents will feel that their controlling behavior is in the best interest of the family. They are convinced that the survival of the family depends on their taking control. Unfortunately, they are often doomed to feel unfulfilled and dissatisfied with the relationship and themselves.

The codependent is, in essence, living his/her life through another. The sense of personal identity, of actually discovering who you are, is sacrificed unwittingly for a compulsive and repetitive learned behavior. The feeling of being consumed by another's needs often leads to depression.

Loss of self occurs when I need your approval and lose the opportunity to think my thoughts and to feel my feelings. I start to live the eternal life instead of internal life. I become outer-directed and not inner-directed, and over time the space inside becomes less and less. I feel less than, and my self-esteem is diminished. I look to you to define me, to direct me, to approve of me, to fix me and, lose more and more of me until I feel empty. What develops is the false self, and that is codependency. When I focus on getting your approval, I lose the approval of self, which is the power that self-esteem gives me. In losing my power, I lose me. I lose my voice. I lose me.

Loss of self occurs when I am focused on fixing, helping, understanding, caretaking you and not on caring about me. For me to not lose self, I need to care about you, not for you. My job is to care about me. I need to feel with you, not for you. You are responsible for feeling your feelings not me. I need to be responsible to you as my parent, spouse, child, or friend, not be responsible for you. I am responsible for me and to you and, you are responsible for you and to me. If we can do this in a relationship than both of us, have the opportunity to mature and to develop a sense of self.

Loss of self occurs when I say "no" when I mean, "yes" and when I say, "yes" when I mean "no." Of course, this sounds confusing, and the codependent often does feel confused, indecisive, and rattled. One can understand why! It is a lifetime of guessing what somebody else needs and wants and over time, the codependent forgets who he or she is. The sense of self is not developed. The individual does learn what he or she needs, wants, feels and the struggle of discovery is absent. Gradually, initially, however, bit by bit, little by little, year by year, the erosion occurs. It is not even the erosion; instead, it is the not building of self, so a double loss is occurring. You miss the journey. Giving out and not putting in is a bad investment whether it is about finances or relationships.

Loss of self is learned helplessness. Reinforced codependent behaviors do not serve me well, nor do they serve others well. Codependent relationship dynamics create and foster dependency for both individuals. It is a no-win dynamic. It is not about individual or relationship building. I cannot give up me and think there can be we. An "I" is needed for a "We" to exist.

Loss of self creates a victim mentality — a victim who cannot see how he or she has built his or her prison. Denial, anger, shame, guilt, passivity, fear, and sadness and often depression, are the bars of this prison. The wounded child and critical parent are present, and the adult ego state has yet to be built.

Loss of self affects the family members and friends of the codependent. Often, the codependent moves from one crisis to the next and others suffer. Denial is a core symptom for the loss of self. Codependent thinking is if I do not see it, acknowledge it, believe it, then it does not exist.

- Are you codependent? Do you have loss of self?

- Do I care for you instead of about you?

- Do I own responsibility for you and not to you?

- Do I need your approval and do not know my mind?

- Do I think for you and do not know my thoughts?

- Do I have appropriate emotional boundaries with you?

- Do I practice emotional detachment with you?
- Do I feel and act like a victim in relationships?
- Do I have low self-esteem?
- Do I repress feelings and have a wall of denial around me and in my relationships?

Codependency is real. It exists within self and relationships. Loss of self occurs as we have just described and it is destructive to self and others. A closing thought is when there is not enough of me for me; surely there cannot be enough of me to share with you. Codependency kills. Codependency is a loss of self. If after reading this article, you see yourself as codependent then reach out for help.

Codependency - Who Am I without Others?

When you find yourself obsessed with someone, walking on eggshells to keep someone you care about from leaving or trying to figure out how to keep someone safe from themselves, you may be experiencing signs of codependency. Codependency is an uneasy kind of love where one's true feelings and needs become secondary to someone else's. It often results in unhappiness, frustration, and exhaustion instead of closeness and understanding.

What is the difference between codependency and just caring a lot about someone? I define codependency as the habit of avoiding oneself by focusing on another person. When one has a codependent relationship, healthy love, respect and trust are compromised. If a codependent pattern has gone too far, establishing an important relationship on better footing may seem almost impossible.

Codependency is often a pattern that develops over time, so it can be hard to see. It is also reinforced by occasional payoffs - both on the conscious and unconscious levels. Conscious payoffs may include feeling needed and useful. And you need not feel alone, even when you are because that other person is on your mind. Other conscious payoffs may include the experiences of infatuation or drama, which can give rise to feelings of romance or excitement that one might be afraid would otherwise pass them by.

Unconscious roots of codependency run deeper. Sometimes, people develop codependency as a life-long strategy of handling fear and trauma by focusing on others. In some families, about the only positive attention a child gets is when they are useful and undemanding. As adults, these people often end up caretaking others beyond what is useful to either person. A person who is frequently criticized and judged at any age can become vulnerable to believing that they are not worthy of their support and attention. These are just a few of codependency's causes.

Ultimately, the worst thing about codependency is that it puts you in the backseat of your own life.

To be in the backseat of one's own life means that one's natural talents and abilities may not be fully realized or even recognized. Because codependency is draining, codependent people may find that they do not have the energy or confidence they need to carry out personal goals, including finding the kind of love they deserve. The habit of focusing too much on others means that ultimately, a person will miss taking charge of the only thing anyone can take charge of - their own life.

If you think you may have codependent leanings, you are not alone. If you feel stuck in codependent patterns with someone you care about, there is a silver lining: because codependency is a habitual state, it can be changed. Although this self-stifling pattern may not dissolve overnight, there are many tools available if you are serious about freeing yourself from it.

First, it is very important that you find supportive people that you can trust to help you break the codependency habit. To try to break this kind of habit just by reading about it is like trying to learn to swim without getting into the water. Find supportive friends and family with whom to talk. Also, it can be helpful to work with a therapist who understands codependency to develop a greater understanding of not only what you want to change but how you plan to get there. You may also want to attend group therapy, or try 12-step groups like Co-dependents Anonymous (CoDA) or Al-Anon. Groups like these can be motivating because you will find people there who are already working on issues similar to yours.

Here are some other tools to help you to free yourself of codependency:

* Keep a journal. Write about what you are grateful for, what you want out of your life, and what is stopping you. Self-focus is easier when you can see your thoughts on paper.

* Pleasing yourself has its reward. Remember what activities or hobbies you like and do them - even if no one else in your life wants to do them with you.

* Become more aware of your inner world. Take time from your day to contemplate and meditate. If you remember your dreams at night, write them down.

* Take a relationship inventory. Who in your current life makes a better or a worse person out of you when you are with them? You don't have to be someone's friend just because they want you to be. Seek out people who help you to grow inwardly.

* Stop "enabling" others. If someone you are helping is not improving, check in with yourself. How do you feel - are you worried or resentful? Are you "help" really helping?

* Avoid the payoffs of codependency, such as approval for doing more than your share, or getting sucked into drama and infatuation. These are inner enemies. Note what feelings different people and places bring up for you.

* When you find you are obsessed, take time and space away from the person or thing you are obsessed with. Setting interpersonal boundaries can help to put your focus back on yourself. Generally, others will respect you more for it as well.

* Develop a sense of spirituality. This can be as simple as appreciating nature, focusing on a hobby or talking to a wise person. Developing a concept of having a higher power within yourself that has answers for you is also helpful.

The most important tool in all of this is that you think well of yourself. This may feel awkward or even like you are just pretending at first. It is critically important to making progress. One of the most heartbreaking things is to watch a codependent person trying so hard to fix things, only to fail and then turn on themselves. People can treat themselves much more harshly than anyone else would. Codependency and low-self-esteem go hand in hand so let go of that inner voice that says you can't change. The beginning of recovery can be just as simple as allowing oneself to begin to see what is good and true about oneself.

Codependency - Being Dependent on Other's Dependency

You take care of others; you help, you go out of your way for...but when do you cross the line from being a compassionate friend or partner or family member to being "codependent"? There may not be a simple test or a clear marker, but if you consistently put someone else's needs first, to the detriment of your own, you may be codependent with your friend or partner, etc. This pattern may be an example of enabling - your behavior helps maintain someone else's destructive or dependent behavior.

A simple example of enabling might be your calling in sick for your husband when he is too hungover to go to work. Codependency may be a justification for allowing yourself to be mistreated based on your low self-esteem - your sense that you don't deserve better. On one end of the continuum, examples might be remaining in a relationship that doesn't support you or your personal growth, while on end, codependency might mean not being able to leave a relationship, even when you are being abused emotionally and physically.

Codependency involves behaviors that go above and beyond normal caretaking behaviors, or the everyday kind of self-sacrificing that happens within relationships. Some examples that are common in people who struggle with codependency include:

Denial patterns, such as having difficulty identifying your feelings, or minimizing how you feel;

Low self-esteem patterns, such as judging yourself harshly and believing you are never good enough or feeling unable to ask others for help;

Compliance patterns, such as compromising your values and integrity to avoid rejection, or staying in harmful situations for too long; and

Control patterns, which include believing that others are incapable of taking care of themselves, or need to be needed to have a relationship with others.

It is important to note that there are criticisms of the label "codependent." For example, caring for an individual with an addiction is not necessarily synonymous with pathology. To name the caregiver as a codependent responsible for the endurance of their partner's negative behaviors can pathologize caring behavior. You may only require assertiveness skills and the ability to place responsibility for negative behaviors on the other person. Also, when this idea is pathologized, the codependent person may swing from an extreme of excessive sacrifice to an extreme of excessive assertiveness or selfishness and an aversion to empathy, which is a positive human capacity. A healthy approach would be to develop a sense of balanced and healthy assertiveness, which still leaves room for caring and helping.

Tendencies and behaviors that can be identified as codependent frequently emerge from a childhood in a dysfunctional family; perhaps one or both parents were alcoholic or had some other profound problems, so these patterns have deep roots. For this reason, codependency may show up in a wide range of your relationships including work relationships and friendships. Some people find 12-step groups such as Al-Anon/Alateen or Codependents Anonymous helpful, although some people do not. Therapy can be a useful tool to help you understand the complexities associated with these patterns and to help you balance your own needs against those of others.

Codependence in Your Life

People that are codependent have grown up in homes in which their parents relied too heavily on each other for emotional support. They watched in disgust as their parents cheated on each other and mistreated each other in other ways. They stayed together long past the point when they should have called it quits. From this experience, the child learned that they were incapable of making it as a healthy and independent adult. The codependent unconsciously think they can't make it without a mate, they are worthless without a mate, and that they are not good enough, along with a host of other negative thoughts. Consciously, they may vow not to become their parents.

The codependent and their love relationships

These people are drawn to relationships that start hot and heavy. Because of their strong need to bond with another individual, they often get seriously involved early on in the relationship. Their mate, who is usually also a codependent, is always available, loving, and affectionate in the beginning. This is a dream come true for the codependent who constantly craves attention. This is until they begin to feel suffocated by their mate's possessive and jealous personality. They take up all their free time and isolate them from their friends and family. Their mate may demand too much not only emotionally, but also financially and mentally as well. The codependent thinks they are in love, although they soon become miserable, lonely, and depressed. To other people, it may appear that this couple is in love because of the amount of time they spend together and the length of time the relationship can continue. If they should split apart, they soon get back together. Healthy men can be attracted to the dependent personality. However, they are just as quickly turned off by their clingy personality and disappear, or they may stick around to take advantage of their generous ways.

Codependents and their interaction with family and friends

But, they tend to be very self-absorbed. They ignore other people's wants and needs to get what they want and need. They are short-term thinkers who constantly seek instant gratification. The codependent doesn't mean to hurt anyone. But, they are often too involved with holding on to their waning relationship to give their family and friends the love and attention they deserve. Their family will always be here, they may be thinking, but they may secretly know their relationship will not be. It is also a possibility that they are too ashamed of who they have become within their relationship to show their face. If the codependent is not involved in a love relationship, they may behave similarly with their family and friends. They may keep too close of an eye on their children and prevent them from hanging out with their friends. They may seem to be mean, but they are desperate not to be alone. When hanging out with their friends, the codependent may get upset when their friends invite someone else along. They can also be too loyal to their friends.

When the codependent tries to become more independent

Once the codependent tries to stand on their own two feet, their mate may become afraid that they will get left behind. Desperate to hold on, they may become violent, verbally abusive, and manipulative. Sometimes codependents halt their growth because they are afraid they will outgrow there mate or because they are afraid to start over.

Codependents at work

It can be hard for the codependent to function at work due to their constantly changing emotions. And, because of the tumultuous nature of their relationship, they often have to quit coming to work or call out often due to family emergencies. Without an attachment, they are very capable of doing a good job at work and making wise decisions. However, they tend to allow themselves to be mistreated by their coworkers and supervisors and they may neglect to ask for raises or promotions because of their self-esteem issues.

Codependence: The Flip Side to Narcissism

The flip side to Narcissism is Codependence. Some codependent traits include A lack of self-direction; looking for reassurance, encouragement or approval before you take on a task or set out to achieve a goal for yourself, often seeking this from people the least likely to give you this support. You feel responsible for other people's feelings or bad moods. You expect your loved ones to guess or interpret your needs when you are upset rather than communicate them directly.

The most common cause of Codependency is growing up with a childish parent. Codependency traits may begin when a child is expected to become caretaker to an emotionally demanding or needy parent where they were made responsible for keeping their parent(s) happy. If either of your parents were irresponsible, childish, an alcoholic, a gambler, unfaithful or abusive, you may have learned Codependency to survive. You may have been made to feel special for taking care of them and being treated more like an adult than a child, but this was at the expense of your own emotional needs and development.

This role may have won you a special favor, but probably felt very uncomfortable. A child's needs and personality have little room for expression or growth in this kind of relationship. You also may have learned some unhealthy ideas about happiness and personal goals.

If you have Codependent tendencies, narcissistic behavior will be extremely confusing and hurtful for you to live with. You probably grew up working hard to please people and confusing this for love. A person who once loved you, but is now irresponsible and points to you as the cause of their problems inflicts an incredible amount of confusion and emotional pain.

But you don't have to stay Codependent forever! There are strategies and tools to start you on having healthier, happier and more satisfying relationships.

Codependency and How It Affects Individuals

A common definition of codependency usually comprises the kind that often affects romantic relationships. One partner will do everything he or she can to please his or her partner, while the spouse takes advantage of these actions to the point of getting the codependent partner bend over backward, sacrificing his or her health, emotion, and income. If left neglected, the codependent partner may grow other dreadful side effects, such as anxiety state, PTSD, depressive disorders, or suicidal tendency. Another definition of codependency involves controlling codependents. Controlling codependents feel they must control the lives of others by dictating their every move. Typical signs of controlling codependents include determining for the other spouse where to go, what to eat, or what to put on. Often he or she will not allow the partner to visit family and friends.

Controlling codependents usually feel that they must manage everything because their partner wouldn't be able to function without them. While the definition of codependency frequently falls under romantic relationships, the fact of the matter is that you may also notice it in platonic relationships also. Quite often the relationships between parents and child are codependent as well. A common example of this includes parents who always sacrifice for their child's every choice to the point where it compromises their health or sanity. As stated by the definition of codependency, these intuitions often stem from childhood abuse in dysfunctional families. Once their parents exhibit neglect or cruelty, children learn to try and predict what their parents choose. This is a defense process that can significantly affect relationships when they grow up. If the definition of codependency sounds familiar, it's time to consider getting help. Institutions such as Codependents Anonymous are excellent for aiding you through this distressing situation. Their twelve phase program allows you to test yourself and your relationship toward others in a manner that will help you to learn why you behave the way you do. Counseling and group therapy are other alternatives you can think about. The truth of the matter is that you don't need to live through these problems alone. By getting help and overcoming your codependency, you will be doing your part to live a healthier, fuller life. Learn more today!

CHAPTER 2

CHARACTERISTICS AND SYMPTOMS OF CODEPENDENT PEOPLE

Are You Codependent?

Do you wonder if you are Codependent? Do you regularly sacrifice your opinions, needs or wants, and then feel resentful? Do you feel guilty saying no and resentful when you don't? Are you controlled by, or try to control someone else, whom your thoughts and feelings revolve around, as in the Barry Manilow song, "I'm glad when you're glad, sad when you're sad?" Are you afraid of speaking up? Resentment, guilt, control, and fear are the hallmarks of codependency; a term once used only to describe the enabler of an alcoholic is now more generally applied to an unhealthy dependency.

Melody Beattie in Codependent No More describes a codependent as: "A person who has let someone else's behavior affect him or her and is obsessed with controlling other people's behavior." John Bradshaw, author of Healing the Shame that Binds You, says, "Internalized shame is the core of codependency." Expert and author of numerous books, Earnie Larsen define it as: "Self-defeating, learned behaviors or character defects that result in a diminished capacity to initiate, or participate in, loving relationships." In Facing Codependence, Pia Melody writes, "Two key areas of a person's life reflect codependence: the relationship with the self and relationship with others."

The seeds of codependence are in childhood, when a child has no choice but to accommodate a parent who is controlling, selfish, depressed, addicted, or abusive. Such children don't get the sense that their wants or needs matter. The family may be one of addiction or neglect, where children take on parental responsibilities and lose touch with themselves in the process. On the other hand, a family may seem perfect. The parents give their children the best of everything, but they expect perfection or adhere to rigid rules and beliefs, leaving no room for individuality and self-expression to flourish.

Codependents usually do all the giving in relationships. Caring and helping others is fine, but if it's at the expense of oneself, or if you don't believe you have a choice - that it would be selfish not to, or you'd risk losing the relationship - then care to take is not just a behavior, it's an identity and source of self-worth. Alice has a big heart and a string of failed relationships. When she likes a man, she gives more than she gets. She helps her them with whatever their problem is. The men take her for granted or feel smothered and eventually leave.

Codependents learn in childhood to attune to the needs and moods of a parent, so much so that they usually don't know what they want or need. Others' needs, desires, and definition of reality take precedence over their own. Sometimes, they don't even know what they think or feel and have difficulty describing themselves. When asked, they shift to talking about family members or their job.

A codependent conversation sounds like this:

Him: "Where would you like to eat?"

Her: "What do you feel like?"

Him: "Whatever you want."

Her: "Do you feel like Chinese?"

Him: "Do you? Would you like Italian?"

You get the picture. Neither person will assert a position. No one will take responsibility for a choice. Maybe, one doesn't want to dine out and rather watch a TV show, but doesn't want to disappoint the other, or is ashamed to admit they can't afford it. Other times, neither knows what he or she wants. Sometimes, an argument starts. It's impossible to problem-solve or compromise if you don't take a position. Issues and feelings are avoided, problems don't get resolved, and resentment builds.

Codependents frequently become obsessed with another person. Their thoughts, motives, and actions begin to revolve around someone else instead of their feelings and goals. Cindy was preoccupied with Nick's health. She oversaw his diet, managed the marketing, and gave him nutrition articles, oblivious to her own health problems.

Codependents may try to control others' feelings and reactions with gifts or flattery, like "buttering up" to be loved, to get what they want, or to keep the peace. They give with an expectation, and when it's not fulfilled, they are not only hurt but also resentful and feel owed. Healthy giving is for the pure joy of it. Because their boundaries weren't respected as children, codependents don't set functional limits with themselves and others. They may be overly invested in someone else's problem or work long hours on the job to the detriment of their family or themselves. They never say no. They may have been taught that it's selfish or "un-Christian" to assert their will, and don't notice that someone else doesn't mind using up their time and resources.

Jane was an accomplished landscape designer, but underbid her projects and spent many uncompensated hours with customers who gabbed away or changed their minds. She was always running behind and resented that she felt constantly pulled by her customers' demands. To her, charging more and setting boundaries was unthinkable.

In an organization, a codependent works harder for less and maybe the "go to" person who'll take the unwanted assignments. Another may be a martyr at home, never asking for help and never heeding her own needs for rest and rejuvenation. Both get satisfaction in being needed and relied upon, but eventually at a price. These women believe they won't be valued if they don't do extra work. Underneath they fear to lose a client, job, or relationship.

Sometimes, one partner appears more needy and dependent, because he or she is possessive, jealous, calls frequently, or constantly seeks reassurance and attention. However, the other partner is also codependent by allowing him or herself to be controlled by these unreasonable demands.

Low-self-esteem is characteristic of codependence. Childhood experiences and messages imprint feelings of being unlovable or unworthy. Codependents are hard on themselves. They push and judge themselves, and often are high-achievers and perfectionists. This sets them up to be in an abusive relationship or one where their needs are not met. They'll tolerate it even despite being attractive, smart, or successful at work because underneath they believe they don't deserve better.

Pointers of Codependency

Codependency usually comes about as your response to another person's chemical dependency. It revolves around your relationships with the people in your life. It involves the effects these people have on you. You, in turn, then try to affect them and their behaviors. As you begin to see them spiraling out of control, you end up trying to control their behavior.

The soul of codependency lays in you, though, not the other person. It is a silent war you begin within yourself. Usually, it develops from low self-esteem. The codependent person does not feel worthy. It is a dysfunctional relationship with the self. Because you live a dysfunctional relationship internally, it manifests externally to others. You don't love yourself, and you don't trust yourself either. You tend to be out of balance and out of harmony. You may feel disconnected. You tend to live life in a reactor mode and give your power over to outside sources.

Chemical dependency is recognized as a disease. Codependency may not be recognized in the same means, but it can make you sick and will not help you or your loved one start on the road to recovery. Codependency is a progressive state. As things around you get steadily worse, your reactions to those things become more intense. In the back of your mind, you may think you are helping the other person. You may have the best intentions. As you see it, they are destroying themselves. You don't realize that the characteristics you portray as a response to their behavior not only sabotage your relationship with that person but sabotage yourself.

Codependents feel obligated to offer unwanted advice to help the other person solve what you see as their problems. You feel responsible for the other person. Somewhere wrapped up in that process you are trying to please others. You want them to see you as necessary in their lives. You want them to see how essential you are to their well being. You will even abandon your routine to help the other person.

When your help is either brushed off or not effective the way, you thought it would be you become angry. You blame others for the spot you are in. You blame others for making you feel the way you do. You feel unappreciated, used and you become a victim. Over time you learn how to endure it. You live with the anxiety, the hurt, and the anger.

If these signs sound familiar, there is a help. Once you have determined that these feelings and tendencies in no way help you or the other person, you must focus on correcting your inclination towards codependency. First, accept that we all are responsible for our feelings and actions. Do not be afraid to let the other person live their life, to live with the consequences they create. Love the person and be there for them, but do not try to control or manipulate the outcome of their behavior. It may be hard at first, but they too have a lesson to learn that you will not always be there to bail them out of their bad choices.

Second, realize that you are worthy of being loved. Don't center your life on other people thinking that you don't deserve happiness too. Stop looking at relationships to provide you all your good feelings. Look within you and start loving yourself. Then others around you will see the radiance you exhibit and will gravitate toward you.

Third, begin to focus on your own life. You have probably let it slide to the wayside. Look for your happiness within yourself, not outside towards others. Think about your passions and what makes you happy. Then start to concentrate on the steps you can take to start living a joyful life.

You may be codependent, but know that you are a strong people. You have just mistakenly focused your attention toward the wrong thing. You have the power to change and to start recovery. That will let you be who you are while letting the other person be who they are.

Symptoms of Codependency

The term codependency has been around for almost four decades. Although it originally applied to spouses of alcoholics, first called co-alcoholics, research revealed that the characteristics of codependents were much more prevalent in the general population than had been imagined. They found that if you were raised in a dysfunctional family or had an ill parent, it's likely that you're codependent. Don't feel bad if that includes you. Most families in America are dysfunctional, so that covers just about everyone, you're in the majority! They also found that codependent symptoms got worse if untreated, but the good news was that they were reversible.

Here's a list of symptoms. You needn't have all of them to qualify as codependent.

Low self-esteem

Not feeling that you're good enough or comparing yourself to others is a sign of low self-esteem. The tricky thing about self-esteem is that some people think highly of themselves, but it's only a camouflage for really feeling unlovable or inadequate. Underneath, usually hidden from consciousness, are feelings of shame. Some of the things that go along with low self-esteem are guilt feelings and perfectionism. If everything is perfect, you don't feel bad about yourself.

People pleasing

It's fine to want to please someone you care about, but codependents usually don't think they have a choice. Saying "No" causes them anxiety. Some codependents have a hard time saying "No" to anyone. They go out of their way and sacrifice their own needs to accommodate other people.

Poor Boundaries

Boundaries are sort of an imaginary line between you and others. It divides up what's yours and somebody else's, and that applies not only to your body, money, and belongings but also to your feelings, thoughts, and needs. That's especially where codependents get into trouble. They have blurry or weak boundaries between themselves and others. They feel responsible for other people's feelings and problems or blame their own on someone else.

Some codependents have rigid boundaries. They are closed off and withdrawn, making it hard for other people to get close to them. Sometimes, people flip back and forth between having weak boundaries and rigid ones.

Reactivity

A consequence of poor boundaries is that you react to everyone's thoughts and feelings. If someone says something you disagree with, you either believe it or become defensive. You absorb their words because there's no boundary. With a boundary, you'd realize it was just their opinion and not a reflection of you and not feel threatened by disagreements.

Caretaking

Another effect of poor boundaries is that if someone else has a problem, you want to help them to the point that you give up yourself. It's natural to feel empathy and sympathy for someone, but codependents start putting other people ahead of themselves. They need to help and might feel rejected if another person doesn't want help. Moreover, they keep trying to help and fix the other person, even when that person isn't taking their advice.

Control

Control helps codependents feel safe and secure. Everyone needs some control over events in their life. You wouldn't want to live in constant uncertainty and chaos, but for codependents, control limits their ability to take risks and share their feelings. Sometimes they have an addiction that either helps them loosen up, like alcoholism, or helps them hold their feelings down, like workaholism so that they don't feel out of control.

Codependents also need to control those close to them, because they need other people to behave in a certain way to feel okay. People pleasing and caretaking can be used to control and manipulate people. Alternatively, codependents are bossy and tell you what you should or shouldn't do. This is a violation of someone else's boundary.

Dysfunctional communication

Codependents have trouble when it comes to communicating their thoughts, feelings, and needs. Of course, if you don't know what you think, feel or need, this becomes a problem. Other times, you know, but you won't own up to your truth. You're afraid to be truthful because you don't want to upset someone else. Instead of saying, "I don't like that," you might pretend that it's okay or tell someone what to do. Communication becomes dishonest and confusing when you try to manipulate the other person out of fear.

Obsessions

Codependents tend to spend their time thinking about other people or relationships. This is caused by their dependency and anxieties and fears. They can also become obsessed when they think they've made or might make a "mistake."

Sometimes you can lapse into a fantasy about how you'd like things to be or about someone you love as a way to avoid the pain of the present. This is one way to stay in denial, discussed below, but it keeps you from living your life.

Dependency

Codependents need other people to like them to feel okay about themselves, and they're afraid of being rejected or abandoned - even if they can function on their own. Others need to always be in a relationship because they feel depressed or lonely when they're by themselves for too long. This trait makes it hard for them to end a relationship, even when the relationship is painful or abusive. They end up feeling trapped.

Denial

One of the problems people face in getting help for codependency is that they're in denial about it, meaning that they don't face their problem. Usually, they think the problem is someone else or the situation. They either keep complaining or trying to fix the other person, or go from one relationship or job to another and never own up the fact that they have a problem.

Codependents also deny their feelings and needs. Often, they don't know what they're feeling and are instead focused on what others are feeling. The same thing goes for their needs. They pay attention to other people's needs and not their own. They might be in denial of their need for space and autonomy. Although some codependents seem needy, others act like they're self-sufficient when it comes to needing help. They won't reach out and have trouble receiving. They are in denial of their vulnerability and need for love and intimacy.

Problems with intimacy

By this, I'm not referring to sex, although sexual dysfunction is often a reflection of an intimacy problem. I'm talking about being open and close with someone in an intimate relationship. Because of the shame and weak boundaries, you might fear that you'll be judged, rejected, or left. On the other hand, you may fear smothered in a relationship and losing your autonomy. You might deny your need for closeness and feel that your partner wants too much of your time; your partner complains that you're unavailable, but he or she denies his or her need for separateness.

Painful emotions

Codependency creates stress and leads to painful emotions. Shame and low self-esteem create anxiety and fear about:

- Being Judged
- Being rejected or abandoned
- Making mistakes
- Being a failure
- Being close and feeling trapped
- Being alone

The other symptoms lead to feelings of anger and resentment, depression, hopelessness, and despair. When the feelings are too much, you can feel numb.

3 Ways to Spot the Damaging Symptoms of Codependency

If you're worried that you might be suffering from codependency, there are a couple of major things to consider when deciding if the concern is warranted. First, ask yourself whether your relationship is based on an addiction-a habit that interferes with your everyday life. It may be surprising, but at its core, codependency is an "addiction" to love and relationships. Codependents frequently lose sleep, have poor eating habits, and an unhealthy social and work life. These symptoms of codependency develop because the addict is too concerned with making his or her partner happy or worrying about the latest conflict. Second, do you have an unequal stake in your relationship when compared to your partner? Codependents tend to make major life sacrifices and are much more devoted to the relationship than their partners are.

Finally, codependents often had awful relationships growing up. This includes rejections and betrayals from many kinds of relationships, even their parents. They see poor relationships as their own fault and grow desperate for love. Look back and see whether you had healthy friendships and family ties growing up. As childhood is such a vulnerable time, it's when negative experiences have the most prolonged effects, which can evolve into symptoms of codependency.

Here are a few more things to think about before checking our codependency quiz:

1. Do you avoid major conflicts by giving in to your partners will?

2. Do you try to control everything and everyone?

3. Do you wish there were an easier way out of your relationship?

4. Are you jealous and possessive?

5. Do you always have to have things perfect and in order?

6. Is it common for you to be insecure in your relationships, including past romances and friendships?

If you have many of these symptoms of codependency, then it's worth exploring whether or not you truly have a problem. Don't despair, though; there is hope for you. Codependency is a very common addiction, and many people deal with it daily.

There are many negative side effects of codependency symptoms. Codependency can lower your self-esteem. Ask yourself whether you value yourself as a person. Codependents often lack a proper sense of self-worth. If your self-esteem suffers, especially in the company of your partner, it's a strong sign of codependency. Beyond damage to your mental health, codependency can also damage relationships. Even though it may seem like your relationships would be safer since you're controlling things to try and make people happy, you're undermining it. Good relationships develop through genuine interaction, which sometimes involves conflict, and this is perfectly healthy and normal. Even though conflict can be troublesome initially, it allows the relationships to grow and strengthen over time.

Symptoms of codependency can lead to emotional crutches we use to struggle along while pretending nothing is wrong. Unfortunately, ignoring a problem doesn't make it go away. Abuse and emotional distress are common in these situations. If you suspect you have symptoms of codependency, a good first step is to further educate yourself about this addiction and come to terms with it. There are many terrific resources out there to help you with this and get you on the road to healing.

Codependency - Identifying Its Causes and Effects

Codependency is a condition brought on by growing up in a dysfunctional family and promoted by our culture. Children whose parents are unable to be fully present with them because they are unable to be fully present to themselves and each other, can be deeply affected. You grow up without seeing how to love with openness and spontaneity, as well as discipline. You gradually turn off your ability to be fully alive. You learn distorted ways to protect yourself from abuse (i.e., core beliefs and coping patterns) that interfere with intimacy.

This process can take place subtly, much like water eroding a rock little by little. Eventually, you adapt by burying your heart and denying that you need your parents' love in the way you do.

Here are some doubts and concerns of clients which reflect the harm that codependency can cause in one's life:

-Did my parents love me? Care for me? If they loved me, why didn't they treat me with more dignity and caring? Why were they so distant, so self-absorbed and sometimes even abusive and violent?

I got burned growing up. My family hurt me so much. Why should I give anyone else a chance to hurt me again?

-I feel drained and my helping others is never enough. I can't fix the problem, and people just get mad at me for interfering.

-Is being intimate something I can learn or am I doomed to feel alone even when I am with others?

-Is it possible to have a good relationship? Sometimes I feel I give my heart, but they want my soul. Recognize energy drainers.

These statements may sound familiar to you. You may have heard them said or said them yourself. They reflect what I call the "Dilemma of Love."

The AMA has recognized codependency as a disease, meaning it has an onset, a progression, and a finality. When you try to take care of unhealthy parents and protect your family system, you have no time to be a child or learn, in age-appropriate ways, how to be an adult. Your feelings and needs are frequently suppressed as they are too threatening. Your emotional growth becomes stunted. Subtly, you learn to play your role, follow the rules, doing what is expected of you. You feel you have to act this way to help your parents and family. Usually, on an unconscious level, you believe that if you truly love your family, you will keep trying to save it. As you continue to abandon yourself, you fall prey to the disease of codependency.

In her book, "Choicemaking," Sharon Wegscheider-Cruse calls codependency...

"... a specific condition characterized by preoccupation and extreme dependence (emotionally, socially and sometimes physically) on a person or object. Eventually, this dependence on another person becomes a pathological condition that affects the codependent in all other relationships." Anne Wilson Schaef has identified this same pathological condition in our society as a whole. She looks at how a society can operate as a dysfunctional system just as a family can.

Codependency now refers to people who are afflicted by their addictive process. They may come from families in which there were no noticeable addictions. Everything may have looked fine on the surface, but the parents were emotionally unavailable to the children and each other. Because addiction is built into our society, most people, regardless of their family background, need to recover from some form of addictiveness.

The prefix "co" in the term codependency means "about" an addictive process. It reflects the reality, recognized by clinicians that a family of addictive disorders exists that includes alcoholism, drug addiction, gambling, sex addiction, and compulsive spending as well as compulsive deprivations such as anorexia nervosa, sexual anorexia, compulsive saving and hoarding, and some phobic responses. The most important new insight of all is that the compulsive deprivation of one substance or behavior often balances the excess of another in the same person.

You can become addicted to substances, people, ideas, activities, behaviors or anything that takes away the pain of reality and gives you a sense of personal identity. The addictive process is the same regardless of the addiction. Therefore, to free your heart and become fully alive it is necessary to heal on two levels: to arrest your addictions, as well as to heal your underlying disease of codependency.

As with any other disease, if you do not seek help, your codependency will progress. As you fall prey to addictions and continually live from a false self, you will eventually break down under strain.

Untreated codependency invariably leads to stress-related complications, physical illness, depression, anxiety and eventually death. Fortunately, although it is a chronic and fatal disease, it is also treatable.

It is especially challenging to treat because it can be subtle and insidious. You may have a successful career and look all together on the outside, but feel tense and uneasy on the inside. This can make it difficult for you to seek help. You may not be able to make sense of the way you feel, and you may not see a cause for your pain. Codependents often say, "Everything's fine in my life. I'm married; I've got a family and great kids. I should be happy, but I feel so empty."

It is important for you to understand that you are not at fault for having this illness. It was passed on to you through the generations whether you wanted it or not.

It is possible to suffer from this even if your parents were not emotionally unavailable. This "late onset codependency" appears even if you come from a relatively healthy family but stay with an untreated partner, you find yourself caught up in the abuse cycle of a dysfunctional relationship. This means your partner lives by dysfunctional rules, and you can develop codependent symptoms as an adult. This leaves you vulnerable to developing some degree of codependency. It is not a black or white situation. It is on a continuum.

As with any issue, your responsibility begins once you are aware you may have this illness and begin to research how to treat your problems. At this point, you can begin to recover your power and choose the kind of life you want. There is so much hope today and as I have said, working with a knowledgeable coach/counselor can bring you the freedom to be who you want to be

Recognizing Codependent Behavior

Codependency is a disorder that develops over time. Dysfunctional childhood patterns that interfere with the person's ability to form healthy relationships lie dormant for many years; the problem only surfaces once the person begins to experience adult relationships.

Codependents do not usually recognize that their behavior is unhealthy, and so they go from one unsatisfying toxic relationship to another. These relationships always end in heartbreak without the codependent ever understanding the primary role he or she played in its demise.

Codependents fear vulnerability. They feel undeserving, not worthy of having others meet their needs, so they put themselves in the role of perpetual caregiver. They believe that they must earn love to get it; fear that if they do not measure up to others' expectations, they will be abandoned. Their fear of others' being angry with them and rejecting them largely determines all their actions and reactions within the relationship.

Codependents often they feel like they do not deserve a better relationship than they already have. They fear giving up the false security it provides them, therefore resign themselves to always settling for second best. At the same time that they are feeling these insecurities, codependents may become angry because they are also feeling used and unappreciated by those they are trying desperately to help. When they do attempt to stand up for themselves, they feel guilty because they are taking rather than giving. They become trapped in a maze of heartbreaking confusion and disappointment.

The codependent person does not know that love is not supposed to be painful. I grew up in a drama-laden, angry home where my parents fought constantly. What was so confusing is that they often told my sisters and me how much they loved each other. That made a deep impression on my young psyche; somewhere along the line that twisted message translated into "love hurts." I grew up believing that true love was supposed to be painful; all my adult relationships reflected that way of thinking. Every one of them was drama-laden and traumatic. Crazy as it seems, even as I think back from a healthy perspective, I thought that pain proved the depth of a couple's love and commitment to each other.

Codependents believe that they have to have another person in their lives to survive. What they do not realize is that they have an addiction and the object of their affection is their drug. They believe to the core of their being that what they feel is deep love and that their behavior is loving, but they do not love healthily. What they perceive as love is, in fact, parasitic neediness.

The codependent person must learn to get his emotional needs met without making others dependent on them. He must also learn to give up his job as a people pleaser. The healing process reinforces that taking care of his own needs before the needs of others does not make him a selfish person.

Codependent behaviors prevent us from finding peace and happiness with the most important person in our lives-ourselves. Codependency is a mental health issue that can only be healed if it is recognized. Recovery is about learning to establish healthy boundaries in all areas of life.

Though codependency is an addiction, it is one can be fully recovered from. Once recognized it takes lots of time, patience, and support to heal from. It also takes honest reflection and great determination, but all efforts are worth it.

Great freedom and serenity come with healing. No longer codependent, the person can easily embrace positive feelings like love, happiness, and fulfillment. She can give when she wants to; not out of insecurity or the expectation of others.

Many people enjoy helping and caring for others. The thing to remember in all our relationships is that there should always be balance and compromise.

CHAPTER 3

PROBLEMS AND RISKS ASSOCIATED WITH CODEPENDENTS AND THEIR RELATIONSHIPS

Codependency - A Crippling Relationship Problem

Dependency problems are one of the biggest issues many relationships face. It can take many different forms, from alcoholism to drug reliance to less overtly dangerous problems, like adrenaline addiction or chronic adultery. Fortunately, modern science and medicine may be able to treat many such dependencies, and addicts of all types can start on the road to recovery. Relationships can survive these problems.

What they may not be able to survive is dependency enabled by codependency.

Codependency is an emotional disorder so severe that some experts classify it as a psychological disease. A codependent is a person who is emotionally controlled by someone who has a dependency issue. Some recovery programs refer to these people as enablers, people who encourage the dependent's addictions by making excuses for the behavior, fixing the problems caused by the dependent's addictions, or otherwise relieving that person of the consequences of his or her actions.

It can be almost impossible for an addict to get better when a codependent is throwing up a smokescreen around them. But it's important to understand that a codependent often doesn't engage in this behavior consciously. Rather, they may do it without realizing. Sometimes, they do realize what they're doing but are unable to control it, even going so far as to feel extreme guilt over their actions and expressing a desire to change.

The cause of codependency usually lies in a lack of inherent self-esteem and self-worth in the codependent. He or she looks outward for feelings of adequacy and acceptance, and the relationship with the dependent is vital to establishing his or her worth as a human being. The relationship, therefore, becomes something of a self-sustaining circle: the dependent's addiction is encouraged by the codependent, and the codependent's self-worth is propped up by the dependent. For many people, this is a difficult, even impossible, cycle to break. But neither person can see real development and growth while the unhealthy relationship exists.

It's also important to realize that codependency is not always enabled by a dependency. All that's required is someone with low enough self-worth to look elsewhere for feelings of adequacy and acceptance. If your partner exhibits signs of secretiveness, jealousy, enabling, self-pity, and shame, he or she might be suffering from this dangerous psychological disorder. You should convince him or her to seek medical attention immediately.

Codependency: Effect of Self-Esteem on Relationships

Research has well-established the link between good self-esteem and relationship satisfaction. Self-esteem not only affects how we think about ourselves but also how much love we're able to receive and how we treat others, especially in intimate relationships.

A person's initial level of self-esteem before the relationship predicts partners' common relationship satisfaction. More specifically, although happiness generally declines slightly over time, this isn't true for people who enter a relationship with higher levels of self-esteem. But the steepest decline is for people whose self-esteem was lower, to begin with. Frequently, those relationships don't last. Even though communication skills, emotionality, and stress all influence a relationship, a person's experience and personality traits affect how these issues are managed and therefore have the greatest bearing on its outcome.

How Self-Esteem Affects Relationships

Self-esteem suffers when you grow up in a dysfunctional family. Often you don't have a voice. Your opinions and desires aren't taken seriously. Parents usually have low self-esteem and are unhappy with each other. They neither have nor model good relationship skills, including cooperation, healthy boundaries, assertiveness, and conflict resolution. They may be abusive, or just indifferent, preoccupied, controlling, interfering, manipulative, or inconsistent. Their children's feelings and personality traits and needs tend to be shamed. As a result, a child feels emotionally abandoned and concludes that he or she is at fault-not good enough to be acceptable to both parents. This is how toxic shame becomes internalized. Children feel insecure, anxious, and angry. They don't feel safe to be, to trust, and to like themselves. They grow up codependent with low self-esteem and learn to hide their feelings, walk on eggshells, withdraw, and try to please or become aggressive.

Attachment style reflects self-esteem

As a result of their insecurity, shame, and impaired self-esteem, children develop an attachment style that, to varying degrees, is anxious or avoidant. They develop anxious and avoidant attachment styles and behave like pursuers and distances described in "The Dance of Intimacy". At the extreme ends, some individuals cannot tolerate either being alone or too close; either one creates intolerable pain.

Anxiety can lead you to sacrifice your needs and please and accommodate your partner. Due to basic insecurity, you're preoccupied with the relationship and highly attuned to your partner, worrying that he or she wants less closeness. But because you don't get your needs met, you become unhappy. Adding to this, you take things personally with a negative twist, projecting negative outcomes. Low self-esteem makes you hide your truth so as not to "make waves," which compromises real intimacy. You may also be jealous of your partner's attention to others and call or text frequently, even when asked not to. By repeated attempts to seek reassurance, you unintentionally push your partner away even further. Both of you end up unhappy.

Avoiders, as the term implies, avoid closeness and intimacy through distancing behaviors, such as flirting, making unilateral decisions, addiction, ignoring their partner, or dismissing his or her feelings and needs. This creates tension in the relationship, usually voiced by the anxious partner. Because avoiders are hypervigilant about their partner's attempts to control or limit their autonomy in any way, they then distance themselves even more. Neither style contributes to satisfying relationships.

Communication reveals self-esteem

Dysfunctional families lack good communication skills that intimate relationships require. Not only are they important to any relationship, but they also reflect self-esteem. They involve speaking, honestly, concisely, and assertively, and the ability to listen, as well. They require that you know and can communicate your needs, wants, and feelings, including the ability to set boundaries. The more intimate the relationship, the more important and more difficult practicing these skills becomes.

Codependents generally have problems with assertiveness. At the same time, they deny their feelings and needs, because they were shamed or ignored in their childhood. They also consciously suppress what they think and feel so as not to anger or alienate their partner and risk criticism or emotional abandonment. Instead, they rely on mindreading, asking questions, caretaking, blaming, lying, criticizing, avoiding problems or ignoring or controlling their partner. They learn these strategies from the dysfunctional communication witnessed in their families growing up. But these behaviors are problematic in themselves and can lead to escalating conflict, characterized by attacks, blame, and withdrawal. Walls get erected that block openness, closeness, and happiness. Sometimes, a partner seeks closeness with a third person, threatening the stability of the relationship.

Boundaries protect self-esteem

Dysfunctional families have dysfunctional boundaries, which get handed down through parents' behavior and example. They may be controlling, invasive, disrespectful, use their children for their own needs, or project their feelings onto them. This undermines children's self-esteem. As adults, they too, have dysfunctional boundaries. They have trouble accepting other people's differences or allowing others' space, particularly in intimate relationships. Without boundaries, they can't say no or protect themselves when necessary and take personally what others say. They tend to feel responsible for others' stated or imagined feelings, needs, and actions, to which they react, contributing to escalating conflict. Their partner feels that he or she can't express themselves without triggering a defensive reaction.

Intimacy requires self-esteem

We all have needs for both separateness and individuality as well as for being close and connected. Autonomy requires self-esteem - both necessary in relationships. It's an ability to stand on your own and trust and motivate yourself. But when you don't like yourself, you're in miserable company spending time alone. It takes courage to communicate assertively in an intimate relationship-courage that comes with self-acceptance, which enables you to value and honor your feelings and needs and risk criticism or rejection in voicing them. This also means you feel deserving of love and are comfortable receiving it. You wouldn't waste your time pursuing someone unavailable or push away someone who loved you and met your needs.

Solutions

Healing toxic shame from childhood takes working with a skilled therapist; however, shame can be diminished, self-esteem raised, and attachment style changed by altering the way you interact with yourself and others. Self-Esteem is learned. Sharing at 12-Step meetings is also very beneficial. Learning assertiveness also raises self-esteem.

Couples therapy is an ideal way to achieve greater relationship satisfaction. When one partner refuses to participate, it's nonetheless helpful if one willing partner does. Research confirms that the improved self-esteem of one partner increases relationship satisfaction for both. Often, when only one person enters therapy, the relationship changes for the better and happiness increases for the couple. If not, the client's mood improves, and he or she is more able to accept the status quo or leave the relationship.

2 Biggest Codependent Traps You Might Be Falling Into

The two biggest traps codependents get themselves into are:

•   Codependents depend on another's approval and acceptance

•   Codependents forgive before rehab is completed

Co-dependency is a way of avoiding one's own life by taking on the problems of another. Codependents tend to avoid their own lives by trying to solve the problems of other people.

A codependent person would feel trapped or obligated to stay in a relationship no matter what damage was committed to themselves or others by an abusive partner. Abuse means financial, emotional, physical or sexual abuse.

The easiest place to observe codependency is in relationships where one or both members are abusing drugs, sex or money. One of the partners will feel compelled to remain in the relationship and support the other.

1. Why Do They Depend On Abusers?

A co-dependent's emotional need to help and gain acceptance from an abusive relationship seems illogical at first. An easier way to see why a person would tolerate all the damage and disturbance a loved one creates has to do with survival.

Codependency is about ensuring another life no matter what. It's like a codepedent took on another's life and is trying to continue their lives. Ex: person gets into financial trouble due to cocaine abuse, reckless living, etc. and the co-dependent pays the mortgage, car payments or worse the drug dealers at the door.

Love or obligation to the abusive person is the major justification. Sometimes the abusive person uses coercion, threats, and extortion to demand support. If support isn't given, emotional pleas, upsets, and threats of leaving the relationship are used. Ex: making a supportive person feel guilty if they don't comply with demands for money or support.

Often sympathy for the abuser is used to plead for forgiveness of wrong doings. Apologies and pleadings for forgiveness will be made. Often these pleas are made until the abuser gets what they want. Then they lay off. Promises will be made that won't be kept.

2. Co-dependents Forgive Instead of Rehabilitate

Although the damage has happened before, a codependent will eventually forgive the abuser. Love, emotional outpourings, sex or other 'payoffs' are given by the abuser as a reward or payment for receiving forgiveness.

The need for a codependent for acceptance of the abuser, the promises and emotions are craved by a codependent. A codependent will sometimes use these forgiveness times as opportunities to gain a false upper hand and control over the relationship.

The Codependent needs the abuser or addict to be helpless, in jeopardy, victimized, in trouble, needing help, vulnerable, for the codependent to feel valued or important! Often a codependent will only help enough to keep a person alive but not enough to change their course of destruction.

Ex: pay off the person's debts with only a promise of the abuser to go to an effective rehab. The drug abuser promises but doesn't fulfill their promise. The codependent uses this bad experience to justify them continuing to pay off debts etc. and never get the true addict help.

Admit you've been drawn into a destructive cycle of codependency that is destructive and only leads to eventual disappointment and you'll begin to see the hook. Just because it looks like drug abuser has the problem, doesn't mean you aren't also wearing the problem for them, feeding fuel to their downward drive.

Codependency is a trap. One way to end codependency is to learn about professional intervention support who will help you break your dependency on another. The goal is getting complete rehabilitation.

Codependence: A Manifestation of the Adult Child Syndrome

Those who live with or are closely associated with those who are chemically or alcoholically dependent for their daily functioning can be considered "codependent," because they quickly become "dependent" with and through them. Although the primary person may be considered the one afflicted with the disease, the secondary one or ones, who are usually the children chronically exposed to his or her behavior, adopt a byproduct of it, struggling to keep it together and function as optimally and efficiently as they can in the world after childhood circumstances progressively pulled them apart. Liquor and other substances need not be present.

Indeed, para-alcoholism, an early term for codependence, implies that a person's actions are driven by the unresolved, painful emotions and fears he was forced to shelve to survive the unstable and sometimes detrimental effects of being raised by the alcoholic himself.

Origins, Definitions, and Manifestations of the Disease

The codependent seed is planted when a person turns his responsibility for his life and happiness to either his ego (false self) or others, becoming preoccupied with them to the extent that he temporarily rises above his pain and, in its extreme, can entirely forget who he even is, when he consistently mirrors someone else-in other words, if he looks out here to the other, he will not have to look in there to himself.

"Codependence, (a major manifestation of the adult child syndrome), is a disease of lost selfhood," according to Dr. Charles L. Whitfield in his book, "Co-Dependence: Healing the Human Condition" (Health Communications, 1991, p. 3). "It can mimic, be associated with, aggravate, and even lead to many of the physical, mental, emotional, or spiritual conditions that befall us in daily life.

"When we focus outside of ourselves, we lose touch with what is inside of us: beliefs, thoughts, feelings, decisions, choices, experiences, wants, needs, sensations, intuitions... These and more are part of an exquisite feedback system that we can call our inner life."

In short, a person can sever his connection with his consciousness and consciousness is who he is.

Like expecting a home appliance to operate without plugging it into an electric socket, a codependent may merge with and feed off of another to such an extent that he no longer believes he can function independently.

The origins of the malady are the same as those which cause the adult child syndrome.

"The hallmark of codependency is taking care of people who should have been taking care of you," according to Dr. Susan Powers of the Caron Treatment Centers.

Instead of being self-centered and expecting to get their needs met, children from dysfunctional, alcoholic, or abusive homes are forced, at a very early age, to become other- or parent-centered, meeting their needs, attempting to resolve or fix their deficiencies, and sometimes making Herculean efforts to achieve their love in what may be considered an ultimate role reversal.

If this dynamic could be verbally expressed, the parent would say, "What I can't do, you're expected to do yourself, substituting you for me."

And this reality may well extend beyond themselves, since they are often forced to replace their parents during times that their younger siblings need for them, becoming surrogate mothers and fathers.

In essence, they disregard their own need for a parent and become one themselves. Instead of being nurtured, they cultivate codependence, since it places them on a path that will entail seeking it in others.

"Our experience shows that the codependent rupture, which creates an outward focus to gain love and affection, is created by a dysfunctional childhood... ," according to the "Adult Children of Alcoholics" textbook (World Service Organization, 2006, p. 60.) "The soul rupture is the abandonment by our parents or caregivers... (and) sets us up for a life of looking outward for love and safety that never comes."

This condition is only exacerbated by the same parents who neither support nor permit a child to express or heal his hurts-and may be met with denial or shame if he tries to do so-leaving him little choice but to stuff and swallow them, resulting in a repressed, but the mounting accumulation of unresolved negative emotions. After repeated squelching of a child's observations, feelings, and reactions, in essence, his reality-he progressively disconnects from his true self and denies his crucial inner cues.

Unraveling, he is poised on the threshold that leads from into out-that is, toward others and away from himself, sparking the conflict between his once true and since replaced false self, which manifests itself as codependence.

Forced, additionally, to focus on his parent's moods, attitudes, and behaviors further plant the roots of this condition but become a necessary survival tactic for two primary reasons.

First and foremost, children assume responsibility for their parents' deficiencies and ill-treatment by justifying it, erroneously reasoning that their flaws, lack of worth, and general unlovability are the culprits for the withholds of their validation and acceptance, thus shifting the burden from the ones who should be carrying it to the one who should not.

Secondly, adopting a sixth sense concerning their parents' moods becomes a safety gauge and enables them to emotionally and physiologically prepare themselves for what has most likely become habitual and even cyclical negative confrontations of verbal and physical abuse.

As episodes of "expected abnormalcy," they add insurmountable layers of trauma to the original but no longer remembered one. Unable, then or now, to use the body's fight or flight survival mechanisms, yet still drowned in a flood of stress hormones (cortisol) and elevated energy, they have no choice but to tuck themselves into the inner child protective sanctuary they created at a very young age as the only realizable "solution" to the parental-threatened and -inflicted danger, enduring, tolerating, and downright surviving the unfair power play and "punishment" they may believe is being administered because of "deserved discipline."

Like signals, a mere frown on or cringe of a parent's face may prime the child for the episodes he knows will assuredly follow. So thick can the tension in the air become at these times, that he can probably cut it with a knife?

Part of the wounding, which reduces a person's sense of self and esteem and increases his feeling of emptiness, occurs as a result of projective identification. Volatility charged, yet unable to get to the center of or bore through his emotional pain, a parent may project, like a movie on to a screen, parts of himself on to another, such as his vulnerable, captive child, until that child takes on and identifies with the projection.

Releasing and relieving himself, the sender, (the parent) does not have to own or even take responsibility for his negative feelings. If the recipient (the child) ultimately acts them out after repeated projected implanting, whose emotions now mount into uncontainable proportions, the sender may berate or belittle him for them, in an ultimate out-of-persona dynamic, which transfers emotions from one to the other.

"If we have unhealthy boundaries, we are like sponges that absorb the painful, conflicted material of others sent from their inner life," wrote Whitfield in "Co-Dependence: Healing the Human Condition" (Health Communications, 1991, p. 93). "It is not ours, yet we soak it up.

"(This only causes) the true self to go into hiding to protect itself from the overwhelming pain of mistreatment, abuse, lack of being affirmed and mirrored healthily, and the double and other negative messages from toxic others around it," he noted.

These incidents become breeding grounds for both the adult child syndrome and its codependent manifestation.

"The adult child syndrome is somewhat interchangeable with the diagnosis of codependence," according to the "Adult Children of Alcoholics" textbook (World Service Organization, 2006, pp. 6-7). "There are many definitions for codependence; however, the consensus is that codependent people tend to focus on the wants and needs of others rather than their own. By doing so, the codependent or adult child can avoid his or her feelings of low self-worth... A codependent focuses on others and their problems to such an extent that the codependent's life is often adversely affected."

Part of a codependent's breeding occurs because a child needs his parents for his emotional and psychological development, yet he often dips into a dry well when he connects with them to achieve this goal, emerging dissatisfied, unfulfilled, and almost stung by the negative, rejecting energy. He may implement several strategies to attain what he vitally needs, but will often fail since his parents themselves never received what he seeks because of their own dysfunctional or incomplete childhoods.

If they could be considered profit-and-loss statements, they would most likely show an emotional deficit and, eventually, so, too, will the child, prompting his ultimate outward- and other- focus.

Bombarded with parental blame and shame, a child can quickly believe that he causes others' negative or detrimental actions by his sheer existence as if he were a negatively influencing entity and may carry both this belief and its burden for most of his life.

"As children, we took responsibility for our parents' anger, rage, blame, or pitifulness...," according to the "Adult Children of Alcoholics" textbook (World Service Organization, 2006, p. 7). "This mistaken perception, born in childhood, is the root of our codependent behavior as adults."

Dr. Charles L. Whitfield uncovers an even deeper cause.

"The cause of codependence is a wounding of the true self to such an extent that, to survive, it had to go into hiding most of the time, with the subsequent running of its life by the false or codependent self," he wrote in "Co-Dependence: Healing the Human Condition" (Health Communications, 1991, p. 22). "It is thus a disease of lost self-hood."

"... The child's vulnerable true self... is wounded so often that to protect (it), it defensively submerges (splits off) deep within the unconscious part of the psyche," he also noted (p. 27).

This split, one of the many detriments of codependence, arrests this development, as his inner child remains mired in the initial trauma that necessitated its creation. Although his chronological age may advance, his emotional and psychological progress remains suspended, creating the adult child. His body and physical statue may suggest the first part of this "adult" designation to others, but his reactions may more closely approximate the second "child" part of it.

Conflicted, he may engage in an internal battle he does not entirely understand, as his adult side wishes and needs to function at an age-appropriate level, but his child half clings to the sting of his unresolved harm, seeking sanctuary and safety. He is unable to satisfy both.

People naturally seek relief from pain and addictions and compulsions, the second manifestation of codependence, is one of the methods they employ, especially since they lack any understanding about their affliction. Because they spark the brain's reward system, however, they only provide temporary, fleeting fixes, not solutions.

Exacerbating this dilemma is the fact that they flow from a false sense of self, which itself can only be mollified, quelled, or deceptively filled by these means.

Since their childhood circumstances were both familiar and normal to them, they subconsciously may also attract, now as adult children, those with similar upbringings using sixth-sense intuitions or identifications, creating a third codependent manifestation.

"... On (an even) deeper level," according to Whitefield in "Co-Dependence: Healing the Human Condition" (Health Communications, 1991, p. 54), "they may also be drawn to one another in a search to heal their unfinished business and, perhaps more importantly, their lost self."

Nevertheless, inter-relating with others who themselves function from the deficit-dug holes in their souls, they only re-create the childhood dynamics they experienced with their parents, substituting their partners for them and suffering a secondary form of wounding over and above the primary one sustained in childhood. In effect, they become another link in the intergenerational chain.

Even if they encounter whole, loving people, who can provide the needed acceptance and validation they crave, they are unable to accept it, since they do not function from the true self that otherwise could-nor, in the event, do they even believe that they deserve it. It bounces off of them like an image on a mirror, only creating yet a fourth byproduct of codependence.

Aside from the codependent foundation laid in childhood by dysfunctional parents, who themselves were wounded and caused the adult child syndrome upon which its codependent aspect was based, the condition is far more prevalent in society than may at first be apparent. Continually, but sometimes subtly modeled, it can almost be considered contagious.

Identifying Codependence:

One of the frustrating aspects of codependence is that it either wears a disguise or remains altogether hidden, prompting the behavioral modifications and almost-scripted roles of those who suffer from it, such as rescuer, people-pleaser, perfectionist, overachiever, victim, martyr, lost child, comedian, mascot, bully, and even abuser, that deludes others to the fact that it is present. The motivation for such behavior is not always immediately apparent.

Nevertheless, there are several traits which characterize codependence.

Sparked by the need to protect the traumatized inner child and to arise, in part, from disordered relationships, it results, first and foremost, in the creation of the false self, which replaces the genuine, intrinsic one, and becomes the root of all other addictions and compulsions. The emptier a person feels inside, the more he seeks to fill that void outside.

"Codependence is not only the most common addiction," according to Whitefield in "Co-Dependence: Healing the Human Condition" (Health Communications, 1991, pp. 5-6), "it is the base out of which all our other addictions and compulsions emerge. Underneath nearly every addiction and compulsion lies codependence. And what runs them is twofold: a sense of shame that our true self is somehow defective or inadequate, combined with the innate and healthy drive of our true self that does not realize and (cannot) express itself. The addiction, compulsion, or disorder becomes the manifestation of the erroneous notion that something outside ourselves can make us happy and fulfilled."

And underlying codependence is a shame and a deep belief that the person is inadequate, incomplete, and flawed.

Avoiding his negative feelings and painful past, he becomes externally and other-focused, yet is unable to genuinely connect with them, with himself, or with a Higher Power of his understanding through the false or pseudo-self, he was forced to create. This has the opposite or repelling effect.

His boundaries, another aspect of the disease, may be distorted, undefined, and extend beyond himself.

Finally, as a defense, codependence is learned, acquired, progressive, and inextricably tied to the adult child syndrome, since the false self serves as the link between the two.

Codependence and the Brain:

Codependence is both additive and breeds addictions. People's actions are usually motivated by rewards and, in this case, the reward is the temporary disconnection from their painful pasts by focusing on others and the belief that doing so will bring them happiness and fulfillment, as they attempt to avoid their emptiness and negative self-feelings.

Although they feel flawed because of their upbringing, the real flaw is that an external source can fill and replace an internal one. The more they look toward others, the more they deny and disconnect from their own needs, wants, and deficits.

"This love deficit condemns us to existence of addiction, para-alcoholism, codependence, or seeking some other outward source to heal an inward feeling of being unwanted or defective," according to the "Adult Children of Alcoholics" textbook (World Service Organization, 2006, p. 438).

Although certain strategies can temporarily relieve their adverse condition, such as avoiding, depending, obsessing, and compelling, excessive reliance upon them, as ultimately occurs with codependence, exaggerates them and elevates them to addiction levels, transforming their "benefits" into deficits. Doing so is not a solution, since it fails to address the underlying reason for it and only ends up creating what can be considered a byproduct problem.

The more a person seeks gratification to rise above his unresolved past, the more he reinforces the neuro-pathway to pleasure in his brain, cementing the belief that this "other-person" addiction can provide satisfaction through external means-so much so, in fact, that the moment his "fix" is removed or is even threatened to be removed, he crashes and falls back into his pit of pain.

Like all addictions, however, it affects not to end there: indeed, the brain eventually creates a tolerance for them, demanding ever greater quantities, frequencies, and intensities to satisfy him, until he becomes that proverbial binary star, orbiting around others, unable to function without them, as he becomes nothing more than his mirror image.

"Just as we develop a tolerance to the effects of chemicals, we develop a tolerance to the effects of our behaviors... ," according to Sharon Wegscheider-Cruse and Joseph Cruse in their book, "Understanding Codependency: The Science Behind it and How to Break the Cycle" (Health Communications, 2012, p. 33). "This vicious, one-way circle is a trap that ends in depression, isolation, institutions, and sometimes death."

Excessive psychological and emotional reliance on others is, in essence, an exaggeration of normal personality traits and can ultimately disable a person, culminating in the disease of codependence. The way the body can quickly become dependent upon mood-altering chemicals, it can equally become physically dependent upon behaviors to the point that compulsions serve as his armament.

"The disease of codependency can be seen as a personal struggle with a variety of compulsive disorders," Wegscheider-Cruse and Cruse wrote

(Ibid, p. 131). "People… have lived in a condition of denial, distorted feelings, and compulsive behaviors, and as a result, they have developed low self-worth, deep shame, inadequacy, and anger."

But the codependent erroneously believes two mistruths. One is that he is intrinsically flawed and the other is that someone outside of himself can fill what he already possesses inside of himself.

Recovery

Problems can be painful, but can often point to solutions-or, at the very least, that they need to be sought.

"Rather than being simply an escape from reality," wrote Whitfield in "Co-Dependence: Healing the Human Condition" (Health Communications, 1991, p. 98), "codependence is also a search. It starts as a search for happiness and fulfillment outside ourselves. After repeated frustration, it ultimately becomes a search for inner wholeness and completion."

Unless recovery is undertaken, usually through therapy and twelve-step program venues, and understanding is achieved, the mistreatment, dysfunction, and abuse that causes a person's early wound and transforms him into an adult child will only perpetuate, suppressing, paralyzing, or altogether removing the tenets of positive emotions, trust, and love needed for healthy human life and increasing the chances of its byproduct, codependence, by placing him on the fruitless path of looking outside of himself for fulfillment until it reaches addiction levels.

"Recovery involves re-accepting and honoring your individuality," according to Dr. Susan Powers of the Caron Treatment Centers.

You are you, as created, and not the image of what others will have you be attained using unhealthy attachments.

Desensitizing traumas, resolving core issues, and progressively regaining trust leads to the gentle recovering of your true or authentic self, enabling it to express itself and provide the internal fulfillment that was always present, but was distorted and deflated through childhood wounding.

Narcissists are also Codependents

Writers often distinguish narcissists and codependents as opposites, but surprisingly, though their outward behavior may differ, they share many psychological traits. Narcissists exhibit core codependent symptoms of shame, denial, control, dependency (unconscious), and dysfunctional communication and boundaries, all leading to intimacy problems. One study showed a significant correlation between narcissism and codependency. Although most narcissists can be classified as codependent, the reverse isn't true - most codependents aren't narcissists. They don't exhibit common traits of exploitation, entitlement, and lack of empathy.

Dependency

Codependency is a disorder of a "lost self." Codependents have lost their connection to their innate self. Instead, their thinking and behavior revolve around a person, substance, or process. Narcissists also suffer from a lack of connection to their true self. In its place, they're identified with their ideal self. Their inner deprivation and lack of connection to their real self make them dependent on others for validation. Consequently, like other codependents, their self-image, thinking, and behavior is other-oriented to stabilize and validate their self-esteem and fragile ego.

Ironically, despite declared high self-regard, narcissists crave recognition from others and have an insatiable need to be admired - to get their "narcissistic supply." This makes them as dependent on recognition from others as an addict is on their addiction.

Shame

Shame is at the core of codependency and addiction. It stems from growing up in a dysfunctional family. Narcissists' inflated self-opinion is commonly mistaken for self-love. However, exaggerated self-flattery and arrogance merely assuage unconscious,

internalized shame that is common among codependents.

Children develop different ways of coping with the anxiety, insecurity, and hostility that they experience growing up in dysfunctional families. Internalized shame can result despite parents' good intentions and lack of overt abuse. To feel safe, children adopt coping patterns that give arise to an ideal self. One strategy is to accommodate other people and seek their love, affection, and approval. Another is to seek recognition, mastery, and domination over others. Stereotypical codependents fall into the first category, and narcissists the second. They seek power and control of their environment to get their needs met. Their pursuit of prestige, superiority, and power help them to avoid feeling inferior, vulnerable, needy, and helpless at all costs.

These ideals are natural human needs; however, for codependents and narcissists, they're compulsive and thus neurotic. Additionally, the more a person pursues their ideal self, the further they depart from their real self, which only increases their insecurity, false self, and sense of shame. (For more about these patterns and how shame and codependency co-emerge in childhood, see Conquering Shame and Codependency.)

Denial

Denial is a core symptom of codependency. Codependents are generally in denial of their codependency and often their feelings and many needs. Similarly, narcissists deny feelings, particularly those that express vulnerability.

Many won't admit to feelings of inadequacy, even to themselves. They disown and often project onto others feel that they consider "weak," such as longing, sadness, loneliness, powerlessness, guilt, fear, and variations of them. Anger makes them feel powerful. Rage, arrogance, envy, and contempt are defenses to underlying shame.

Codependents deny their needs, especially emotional needs, which were neglected or shamed growing up. Some codependents act self-sufficient and readily put others needs first. Other codependents are demanding of people to satisfy their needs. Narcissists also deny emotional needs. They won't admit that they're demanding and needy, because having needs makes them feel dependent and weak. They judge as needy.

Although narcissists don't usually put the needs of others first, some narcissists are people-pleasers and can be very generous. In addition to securing the attachment of those they depend on, often their motive is for recognition or to feel superior or grandiose because they're able to aid people they consider inferior. Like other codependents, they may feel exploited by and resentful toward the people they help.

Many narcissists hide behind a facade of self-sufficiency and aloofness when it comes to needs for emotional closeness, support, grieving, nurturing, and intimacy. The quest of power protects them from experiencing the humiliation of feeling weak, sad, afraid, or wanting or needing anyone-ultimately, to avoid rejection and feeling shame. Only the threat of abandonment reveals how dependent they truly are.

Dysfunctional Boundaries

Like other codependents, narcissists have unhealthy boundaries, because theirs weren't respected growing up. They don't experience other people as separate but as extensions of themselves. As a result, they project thoughts and feelings onto others and blame them for their shortcomings and mistakes, all of which they cannot tolerate in themselves. Additionally, the lack of boundaries makes them thin-skinned, highly reactive, and defensive and causes them to take everything personally.

Most codependents share these patterns of blame, reactivity, defensiveness, and taking things personally. The behavior and degree or direction of feelings might vary, but the underlying process is similar. For example, many codependents react with self-criticism, self-blame, or withdrawal, while others react with aggression and criticism or blame of someone else. Both behaviors are reactions to shame and demonstrate dysfunctional boundaries. (In some cases, confrontation or withdrawal might be an appropriate response, but not if it's a habitual, compulsive reaction.)

Dysfunctional Communication

Like other codependents, narcissists' communication is dysfunctional. They generally lack assertiveness skills. Their communication often consists of criticism, demands, labeling, and other forms of verbal abuse. On the other hand, some narcissists intellectualize, obfuscate, and are indirect. Like other codependents, they find it difficult to identify and clearly state their feelings. Although they may express opinions and take positions more easily than other codependents, they frequently have trouble listening and are dogmatic and inflexible. These are signs of dysfunctional communication that evidence insecurity and lack of respect for the other person.

Control

Like other codependents, narcissists seek to control. Control over our environment helps us to feel safe. The greater our anxiety and insecurity, the greater is our need for control. When we're dependent on others for our security, happiness, and self-worth, what people think, say, and do become paramount to our sense of well-being and even safety. We'll try to control them directly or indirectly with people-pleasing, lies, or manipulation. If we're frightened or ashamed of our feelings, such as anger or grief, then we attempt to control our feelings. Other people's anger or grief will upset us, so that they must be avoided or controlled, too.

Intimacy

Finally, the combination of all these patterns makes intimacy challenging for narcissists and codependents, alike. Relationships can't thrive without clear boundaries that afford partners freedom and respect. They require that we're autonomous, have assertive communication skills, and self-esteem.

If you have a relationship with a narcissist, check out my book, Narcissist: Discover the true meaning of narcissism and how to avoid their mind games, guilt, and manipulation (Mastery Emotional Intelligence and Soft Skills Book 11).

CHAPTER 4

START LOVING YOURSELF AND STOP BEING CODPENDENT

Do You Know Who You Are?

The thoughts we have about ourselves are linked to all the feedback we get from a huge range of sources, take a moment and consider all the people who have had influence on how you think about yourself during your lifetime. My list would comprise of my parents, siblings, teachers, friends, colleagues, employers, previous partners, my children. We all have our ups and downs, moments when we feel fabulous and others when we don't. When we're feeling really good someone may have paid us an unexpected compliment, your partner may have brought you flowers for no reason, your child may have given you a hug just because... this good feeling was caused by an outside influence, but unfortunately this equation also works the other way around but with more punch it seems. If you're not feeling particularly good about yourself maybe a teacher/coach said you weren't good enough, your partner asks if you are going to get dressed for dinner when you are ready to go, your parents asked why you couldn't be more like them?

The interesting thing about this is that we hold onto the negative a lot longer than the positive, even though it makes us feel bad. The comments, for example from your teacher or parents, could have been made years ago, but the positive ones much more recently and yet still the negative comments override the positive ones. If we carry on holding on to negative statements and letting them impact how we feel about ourselves, we are setting ourselves up for misery and constant questioning of who we are and whether we are worth loving.

So you will need some time alone, without distraction, to get to know who you are, this is for no-one else's benefit but yours (at this stage, but we'll get to that).

Here's what I'd like you to write down;

• Your three core values, what are you not negotiable on?

- At least five strengths you have in abundance.

- Your weaknesses, we all have them, be honest with yourself.

- What makes you smile, feel calm, content, satisfied with your life.

- What makes you feel upset, anxious, sad, dissatisfied with your life.

It's not as easy as it sounds, is it? Have you written down what you expected or did taking the time and thinking thoroughly about yourself produce some surprises?

Healing requires that you admit the truth about yourself...

Firstly, your core values, the foundation for who you are and what you stand for. When you are running your life and relationships in line with these, you will feel calm, content and balanced because everything is working in harmony together. When we do or are asked to do something that is not in line with our core values we experience discomfort, anxiety, worry, and unhappiness. For example, your boss asks you to attend an important meeting when you know you have to be at your child's recital, if one of your core values is family, this situation will make you feel very unsettled, anxious and potentially upset.

We have all made decisions at some point that have not been in line with our core values, but maybe we did not understand the reason behind the negative feelings we were experiencing at the time. The key thing to note here is knowledge is power, when we consciously know exactly what our core values are we know to remain calm, content and balanced in our life we must work in line with them.

Steps to Understanding and Accepting Who You Are

Sometimes we lack a realistic view and understanding of ourselves which can lead to feelings of being "lost" in our lives and depression. Understanding yourself helps you to accept yourself the way you are, and in turn, makes you a happier person. You cannot control everything in life, but if you understand yourself and make good choices based on who you are and knowing what you want out of life, you can begin to enjoy life to the fullest.

Here are a few steps to start you on the road of understanding yourself:

Step 1: Accept that you are unique and valuable in your special way, just as you are. We all matter to our close friends and family. You are very important both for yourself and to others.

Step 2: Now you need to dig deep to understand the real YOU, without any pretenses. Set time aside to do this exercise. Explore the way you really feel about yourself, you can start with answering a few questions like:

- What are the fears and beliefs that are holding you back?

- Are you living your life or are you just existing from day to day?

- What makes you truly happy?

- What are the things that you know you can do well?

- What is your self-talk? Negative? Positive?

- Do you treat yourself and others with respect?

- Do you take responsibility for your life or do you feel like a victim of your circumstances?

- What do you want out of life?

In understanding yourself as much as you can, you start to gain confidence in your strengths, and you will also recognize your weaknesses. Rather than shying away from your flaws, you could help yourself better by accepting them and working on them. Build an honest picture of who you truly are. Maybe you can ask close friends and family members, whose opinions you respect, to give you honest feedback on their perception of you and how you interact with them and respond to situations.

Step 3: Once you understand yourself, you can always work to better yourself, but it should be because of what you want to achieve in life and what you expect from yourself, not because you believe it to be what others want from, or expect from you. Remember there is no reason for you change who you are unless you feel it will be beneficial to you and move you in the direction of the way you ultimately want to live your life.

Understanding yourself means being comfortable with who you are and what you are. It also helps you realize your strengths and weaknesses so you can accept and embrace yourself - warts and all.

Love Yourself for Your Own Sake

The love for family and friends is second nature and often taken for granted. It isn't always easy, but there is a foundation that sustains relationships and holds them together through the hardest times. That base grows in the heart and builds on strength from within. Caring about others is what others expect from you, but you must love yourself to make that possible. Take an inner assessment of all that is good about yourself, and appreciate your value. It is the strongest force you possess.

Consider and Assess

Celebrating the good things in life is joy. Making it to the end of a hard day is part of the routine. Supporting loved ones in crisis is a call to duty. There is a soldier in the soul who rises to the best, handles the mundane and responds to the battle call. When too little attention is given to the emotional toll of dealing with everyday ups and downs, the soldier becomes weary. Coping is a survival mechanism, but living well involves more than simply getting through the day. Understand that your inner strength depends on your ability to know, appreciate and celebrate yourself.

Value and Admire

Taking stock of inner worth begins with understanding the inventory of what makes you special. The ability to empathize, an unselfish nature or an artistic touch are not unique traits. However, when channeled through your individuality, a common asset becomes your treasure. It deserves nurturing and sharing. Appreciate all that is good within you. Know that it is the essence of who you are and what you have to offer. Being told the importance of self-worth is as easy as reading a popular book or attending a self-help seminar. Truly believing in yourself only comes from realizing how very special you are.

Develop and Grow

A garden thrives on attention and care, and its beauty comes from its variety of colors and flowers. Develop an inner catalog of your best features, and indulge in cultivating them to their finest. Recognize the accomplishments that bring you the most satisfaction, and make them a part of your daily life. Volunteering once a month at a shelter is satisfying, but sharing your ability to give every day magnifies your generosity and the pleasure you receive from giving. A gift for painting or writing deserves more than a weekend of dabbling. Focus your creative imagination into unusual corners, such as daily problem solving or weekly planning. Celebrate your talents, recognize their power, and treat them with loving care. Always be your own best friend.

The value you place on yourself is a reflection of how well you understand yourself. Cherish the traits and strengths that bring you true fulfillment and sustain inner peace and joy. Nurture your natural abilities, appreciate them, and indulge them. When you take care of yourself first, your capacity to give, share and love become unlimited. Treasure the talents that give you pride and satisfy you. Set aside a little time each day to reflect on your positive attributes, and think about the best way to express your best. Appreciate how much better you are for simply knowing yourself better. Trust your courage, and celebrate how unique you are. No one can love you as well as you can love yourself.

Accept Who You Are

You look around and realize that you are not the same as other people. You may realize that someone else looks better than you. You may see that someone else has better clothes than you or is in better physical shape. Those differences occur because we are all different people. We were made differently, and we need to realize that we are different so that we can love each other's differences. If we were all the same, where would the fun be in that?

Having a positive attitude about life is easier said than done. Some people may have a negative attitude about life because of past experiences. Others may have a negative outlook because things in their lives never turn out their way. Those people might hate who they are and desire to be like someone else. They may give up hope and decide to end it all. Ending it all is a very bad thing to do because that person who ends it all could have been successful; he/she could have saved lives, yet took his/her own.

To increase self-esteem, and thereby prevent suicide, one must accept himself/herself. The first step in learning how to accept yourself is learning how privileged you are. Some people think their situation is the worst situation. However, through one perusal of the news, one might find out that his/her situation is nothing compared to other people around the world. Another way to start accepting who you are is by learning your history. Ask your mom or dad about your past. If they don't know, or if you cannot find out that information, try to find out information about your own history.

Learning your own history means learning the history of people of your ethnicity. Once you learn how people in your culture struggled and overcame struggles in history, you will accept who you are and start loving yourself.

If you don't like history, as many people don't, then focus on the present. Think of the struggle you're going through. For example, if you are a person who is overweight, search online for stories about people who used to be overweight, people who lost the weight. Maybe you could search for people who have stories about how they overcame their internal struggles. Real stories from present-day people are very helpful. While you read those stories, you learn that you're not alone. Other people feel the exact same way you feel. Don't despair, keep trying.

Once you have read the stories, start a goal list. A building is never built roof-down. Therefore, your first goals should be very, very short term. Start with something you can achieve in one minute. For example, make it a goal to read a joke every day. Jokes can be found online. They could be in the form of text, or pictures. You could look up funny pictures, cool short jokes, or you could look up videos of cats playing the piano. Make it a goal to have at least one minute where you laugh each day. After that, you could start a goal that takes an hour per day. Then move onto one that takes a day per week, then one that takes a week per month, then one that take a month per year. Before you know it, your goal to laugh a minute per day has changed into achieving joy throughout the whole year. And if you're joyful throughout the whole year, you will certainly be during the next, and the next.

All this seems easier said than done. However, if you start with a minute's goal and move up, true acceptance of your self is possible.

Self Esteem - 5 Ways to Feel Better about Who You Are

The definition of self-esteem is how you feel about yourself and how you think others feel about you. Do you feel that other people, especially those with influence in your life value, love, and accept you for who you are? If the answer is yes, then you probably have a normal to high self-esteem level. On the other hand, if you have low self-esteem, you may feel a low sense of self-worth and feel incapable of pleasing those around you.

An individual's self-esteem is directly related to his or her self-image. This is the mental picture that you have of yourself based on some factors like how you look, what you can do successfully, and the things that you are not so good at. Because these two are so closely related, as you grow over time and develop new interests and experience new things your self-image will change too. This affects your self esteem in either a negative or positive way.

First, it is important to understand that self-esteem is affected by how you see yourself and how others treat you. For children and even adults, critical parents, teachers, spouses, and bosses all have the power to negatively affect self-esteem. While you may not be able to control others, you can change the things that you think about yourself by first becoming more aware of them.

Take time to reflect on how you are thinking and even talking to yourself so to speak. If you find that you frequently have a negative inner voice, this could be a large cause of low self-esteem.

The good news here is that your self-esteem is not set in stone. You can do some things to improve it:

1. Reverse Your Negative Thought Patterns

If you have discovered that you are your own worst critic, you need to begin to focus on the things that you like about yourself. At first, you might need to be very deliberate about this by writing positive aspects about yourself down in a journal.

2. Set Realistic Goals

Some individuals set standards and goals for themselves that only aim at perfection. And, since perfection cannot be achieved their self-esteem is damaged even further. Set small achievable goals for yourself. Don't forget to congratulate and even reward yourself as you meet your goals.

3. Improve Self Esteem With New Experiences

Try new things including hobbies, sports, and events just because you want to. As you experience success in these areas, your self-esteem will soar.

4. Make Exercise Part Of Your Daily Routine

Exercise will not only give you more energy and increased health; it also releases endorphins that contribute to positive self-esteem. Working out regularly is something you need to make a habit of, even if it is just a walk around the neighborhood.

5. Cut Yourself Some Slack

Some people with low self-esteem are so hard on themselves whenever they make a mistake that they are afraid to ever try something new. Teach yourself to see mistakes as a learning experience. See it as a chance to get better next time.

Self-esteem is important because it can affect every area of your life. Your relationships will thrive or suffer based on how you feel about yourself and how you think others feel about you. Maybe you have heard it said that if you want people to like, then you first have to like yourself. That is exactly how self-esteem works.

Learning to Love Who You Are

It's a true statement to say that we were all born selfish. But it's not a true statement to say that we all were born with the understanding of self-love. Most of us are not aware of just how much we don't love ourselves until we've experienced negative encounters with other people. Is it possible for a person to be selfish and not love who they are? Most definitely! Today, you see a lot of people that proclaim to have self-love, when in fact what you see are people that have had a growth spur in selfishness.

Webster's dictionary defines selfishness as "concerned excessively or exclusively with oneself; seeking or concentrating on one's own advantage, pleasure, or well-being without regard for others." Webster's also defines love as "an unselfish loyal and benevolent concern for the good of another; as the fatherly concern of God for humankind, brotherly concern for others. " Though many equate selfishness with self-love, by these definitions, clearly you can see that they are not!

Learning how to love and accept yourself means taking away all the conditions and mental limitations that would cause you to believe that you don't deserve to be loved or accepted. It may also require you to end unhealthy relationships that will perpetuate feelings of unworthiness and hopelessness. In general, you will have to evaluate those experiences both past and present to help you understand what may have prohibited you from developing in this area of your life. Were you the product of a single parent home? Were you abused mentally, physically or sexually as a child? Were you bullied and humiliated before classmates in school? It's these types of experiences that will develop as a root in a person's life which ultimately bears fruits of selfishness, drug and alcohol addictions, and sexual misconduct.

The first step in learning how to love and accept yourself is to forgive yourself and others for what may have caused a lifetime of pain. Forgiveness is so important because this is where your freedom resides! Your freedom from hurt and pain lies in your ability to forgive those that have hurt you in any fashion. If you allow un-forgiveness to harbor in your heart, you also allow bitterness and brokenness to live there as well. You must forgive others and also forgive yourself for moving forward.

The second step is to observe your actions and reactions concerning life situations. You must learn to be aware of the why behind every decision you make concerning your life. We don't realize most of the time that what we do and how we react to life circumstances says a lot about how we feel about ourselves. Our decisions can shape our views of self and can block our development of self-love. Decisions can be both conscious and sub-conscious. We usually know why we are making a conscious decision to do something; therefore; it's the sub-conscious decisions that get us into trouble. This is why it is important to evaluate the why behind EVERY decision, so you can become more aware of your reasoning.

The third step is to understand that you are unique! There will never be anyone like you in all the years to come! There is something special about you and there is a reason and purpose for why God created you. You have a unique plan purposed for YOUR life. So many times we judge and compare ourselves to other people and this is a dishonor to you. There are certain things you were graced to do and other things you were not graced to do. When we try to cross over into areas that are not our gifts, this can cause a deep sense of dislike towards yourself because you feel that something is wrong with you. Stay in your lane! Don't try to do things that you know you don't have the grace to do.

Developing self-love and acceptance can be a lifelong process for many. But it doesn't have to be if you can identify those areas in your life that continually keep you from personal growth and make peace with them. Decide today that you will learn to love and accept who you are, regardless of your past. Your past can be a great teacher, or it can be a memoir of pain and mistakes that often revisits you leaving feelings of inadequacy. You're more than that! You just have to start believing that you are!

Six Tips for Loving the Fabulous Person You Are

Throughout my life, I've encountered scores of people who don't appear to love themselves. They say negative things about their appearance, their lack of success at work, not being a good parent or child, or not making the right choices in life. While it is true that we all grapple with issues related to any of these items, we should spend more time on itemizing and being grateful for our positive attributes and successes, and less time on what we feel is wrong with us, negative experiences, or perceived failures.

Make list of the things you like about yourself

These items could relate to your physical appearance, your emotional status, your mental acuity, the type of friend or parent you are, how you relate to people at work or any other positive attribute that comes to mind. Add to this list as you identify additional items you like about yourself. Keep this list in a place where you see it daily. It will remind you of your unique strengths, talents, skills, attributes, and gifts.

Make a second list of complements that you have received from family members, friends, coworkers, neighbors, and others.

Again, add to this list every time you receive a compliment if it is different from those already on your list. You will begin to see a pattern of the positive attributes that others see in you. Remember to keep this list in a place where you can review it daily. If you are experiencing difficulty in developing this list, ask people you trust what they love most about you.

Make time for yourself every day,

Even if it is just for 15 minutes. During this time, review your lists. They will remind you of what you and others like about you. This can be uplifting when you are having a rough day. Spending time with yourself can also allow an opportunity for you to examine issues, resolve problems, or recharge your batteries. By allowing yourself this special time, you are taking care of yourself, which is part of loving one's self.

Learn how to enjoy those times when you are alone.

Engage in activities that make you feel good and give you comfort, whether this is watching your favorite TV program, reading a good book, going out to your favorite restaurant, or taking a hot bubble bath. When you can be comfortable in being alone, doing those things you love most, you are showing yourself how much you value you. If you do not enjoy being alone, examine what is behind that. Assess why you need to constantly be around other people. What are you hiding from? What don't you want to face?

If you constantly berate yourself or can't understand how people can love you

You might want to consider counseling or therapy. Whether your issues come from childhood traumas or a series of negative experiences, it is never too late to put the past to rest and move on. We can't change the past, but we can shape our future. A counselor or therapist can help you to see how past experiences have resulted in current feelings and behaviors. Once you understand this and know that you can't change the past, you will be in a better position to move forward and begin exploring ways to appreciate you for the person you are and love yourself.

Spoil yourself, as you deserve it

Pamper yourself by doing what makes you feel good or loved. If it is spending a day at the spa, going on a vacation, or spending time with loved ones, set aside time to do it. Although I think you should spoil yourself daily, make sure you do this at least once a week. And don't feel guilty... you deserve it!

If you are experiencing difficulty in loving yourself, take time to develop a list of your strengths and attributes, take note of the compliments people give you, take time every day to relax and remember what makes you unique, learn how to enjoy your alone time, seek counseling or therapy if you need to work through past issues, and remember to spoil yourself, at least weekly if not every day. You are a loving person and are loved by more people than you can imagine. Learn how to love yourself... you are your most important asset!

Six Pillars of Self Esteem - Accept Yourself for Who You Are

The six pillars of self-esteem are a vital key to success. Self-acceptance is one of the six pillars of self-esteem. If you don't have a good level of self-esteem and self-acceptance then you will find that being successful is more difficult. Your interactions with people will not produce the results you want, you will suffer from poor motivation, and you will drift from day to day running the risk of not facing up to reality.

The six pillars of self-esteem include facing up to facts, being willing to stand up for ourselves, having a purpose, having integrity, and being responsible for our actions.

The last of the six pillars of self-esteem is self-acceptance - being willing to experience who we are even if we don't like what we see. Only a person with high self-esteem can accept themselves for who they truly are. If you want personal growth and personal success, you will need to be able to accept yourself as you are.

A failure of self-acceptance will cost you dearly

Being unwilling to accept yourself for what you can lead you to waste enormous amounts of time and energy trying to be something you are not. In the long run, this effort is usually wasted as you true self comes shining through -warts and all!

While you are busy rejecting our true self, you are increasing our levels of unhappiness, stress, and anxiety. If you have severe difficulty in accepting yourself, the mental consequences can be very serious indeed.

How to accept yourself?

Of the six pillars of self-esteem, self-acceptance is the one that is most closely associated with our past conditioning, and it is most deeply rooted in our very core. Improving your levels of self-acceptance can take time and patience. However, the rewards in terms of personal growth and personal success are very worthwhile.

Very often we have the most difficulty accepting our faults - we seem them as massive mountains when if we could see ourselves as others see us, they would just be tiny molehills. So one thing to do is to get the opinions of people who you trust, to be honest with you and who you know will help you.

On the flip side, if you are the person who does not have the six pillars of self-esteem firmly embedded in your makeup, it is very common to overlook many of your positive qualities in favor of beating yourself up about your weaknesses. Find some time to sit down quietly and think about the successes you've had throughout your life. Identify and write down all the positive qualities that have led to those successes.

Think about people you know well enough to recognize their good and bad sides. That should help you to realize that no one's perfect. If everyone were perfect, the world would be a very uninteresting place. You need some imperfections to highlight your best qualities

Provided your faults don't lead you to be dishonest, immoral, or cause harm to other people, accept that there's nothing wrong with them.

Where your faults have led you to make mistakes, don't beat yourself up endlessly for your perceived failure. Understand that there's no such thing as failure or mistakes; they are just learning experiences. If you can use them to move forward, you will be much better off.

Finally try at all times to make sure that all your actions are aligned with universal principles such as love, mutual respect, honesty, integrity... that way you don't have anything to feel bad about.

Working on the six pillars of self-esteem, which includes working on accepting yourself for what you are, both the good and the not so good is important for you to live a happy and fulfilled live, achieving personal growth and personal success. There are many keys to success that let you come to terms with yourself as you are.

Loving Yourself for Who You Are

One of the major underlying issues in the vast majority of health problems is having a lack of self-confidence. This, in turn, stems from not truly loving yourself for who you are. Women, especially, tend to fall prey to this notion. Because women feel a higher demand placed on them to look and act a certain way while at the same time competing with men for corporate positions and employment, they often are super critical of their body image. Often, when you compliment a woman, she won't take it seriously, thinking that surely you must not see her imperfections the way that she does.

Self-confidence doesn't come wrapped up in a neat package. Rather, it is something that must be learned and ingrained in you. You gain self-confidence by loving yourself and accepting all of your "faults" as being a part of your physical makeup. Sure, there are some things that you can change about yourself such as body image by working out and eating healthier, but other things you cannot do so much to change quite as easily. Even though it sounds sort of cliché, you truly have to love yourself. Part of that means respecting yourself before you can respect others. You cannot truly love other people if you don't love yourself first.

Stress and the demands of a job and a family can put a lot of pressure on you at times. This is why it is important to have other outlets to turn to to relieve stress. Many people, when they are faced with stressful situations put a lot of pressure on themselves. Often, they will be the first ones to blame themselves for things that are often out of their control and for which they had no part of. Having a support system of close friends and family is important when learning how to love and respect yourself. We all need someone to encourage us in times when we are feeling most vulnerable.

Learning how to live a good life is often difficult to do because there are many temptations out there which make it so. By being a good person and doing the right things, we can gain more confidence in ourselves. It is in times when we know that we are not doing the right things to help ourselves or other people that we feel the most guilty. Whenever we make decisions, we need to remind ourselves what is at stake. You need to live a life that you can be proud of. You want to be able to sleep soundly knowing that you made well-thought-out decisions which had positive outcomes.

All of this is part of being a better person. If someone else approaches you and asks you to do something unethical, whether it is a boss, colleague or friend, what will you decide to do? It is a matter of prioritizing what is important to you in your life as well as what you can live with at the end of the day. Learn to see people and situations for what they are worth. Don't sell yourself short, and learn to speak up for yourself. You'll do yourself a favor in the long run, not to mention the fact that you'll do so much more in terms of your personal development as a human being.

Discard Approval, Love and Accept Yourself

Let go of the need for approval and just be who you are and spread love and appreciation around you like there's no tomorrow.

Have you any idea how common it is for people to think about what others think of them?

To be concerned about what others might have thought of them yesterday when they said something that wasn't what everyone else thought? And if they really could do this thing they feel passionate about- what if people laugh at them, or thought they were. well, different?

The truth is that many do think these thoughts while thinking they are the only ones who think them... People are more hung up on what others think of them and haven't even had time to be worried about what you said at all.

The next time you find yourself consumed by thoughts like this; turn it all around and look at the other person as a person who has the very same concerns that you have. How could you give the other some comfort? What would you say to yourself if it was you, (which it is on a deeper level), that wondered if you had said something "stupid" or "wrong"? What would happen if you turned your attention away from your little self and put it instead on the other person and his/her well-being? And what if that other person did the same to you and thought of you first..?

Well, things would be very different between us humans.

Now comes the next step, and it sometimes makes people again think "What will they think of me if I said this or that to or about this person?" It has to change; the fact that it is easier to talk negatively behind someone's back than it is to openly say something positive to someone.

To give someone appreciation for no reason at all, a compliment or a word of encouragement can really scare people, and sometimes you might even get a strange look from someone if you do this openly, especially if you don't have any "reason" for being supportive and "nice." If we only knew how much it could mean to someone else to hear that we matter, or that which we do is appreciated.

Yesterday I listened to a seminar online, and I don't remember which brand or company it was, but it is a famous hair salon. Anyway; the story was that he, the owner, had had a customer who wanted a nice hairdo because she was going away later that evening, so while making her look more beautiful he also said many times that she is beautiful and so on; he gave her compliments and made her feel important. I don't remember the whole story, but the core message was, that the woman had planned to kill herself that evening, and went to the hairdresser to make herself beautiful before she killed herself, but that while being there she changed her mind because of this hairdresser who made her feel beautiful and important.

From that moment on; the hairdresser has trained all his employees to ask within themselves "how can I make your day better?" or something like that to all of their costumes. I thought it was a wonderful story.

Think about the effect a kind word can have! Let us be brave and give compliments and encouragement regardless of what others might think of us.

I have had times in my life when I have asked myself if what I do really has any meaning at all, times when I have felt discouragement, when suddenly I get an email from someone who has been touched by my words, or someone says to me that what I have done for them has helped them to see things differently and therefore helped them to take a step in the right direction.

That has been the sign I needed form God to continue what I do regardless of how things have seemed to evolve.

Today; do something similar for at least three people in your life. Tell them that they matter, tell them that you appreciate what they have done for you. Make them feel important. Or just smile to someone on the street and say "hello."

What I have done for years now is that I send a silent blessing to people I meet or see. When I walk by them, I say "God bless you" in my mind to them, I say "may your day be blessed with joy," "may you always be protected by the Angels" and so on.

I do this every day; it has become a habit, and sometimes I can feel and see they knew something happened, I can see in their eyes that they on some level "heard" and received the blessing. I can feel the love flowing between us, even if we have never seen each other before.

What if we all did that? Wouldn't it be wonderful? It can be done, and it's easy; because it all begins with You.

CHAPTER 5

HEALING AND RECOVERING FROM NARCISSISM AND EMOTIONAL ABUSE

Discover Your Level of Narcissism

All of us have some characteristics and behaviors that fall into the category of narcissism. Narcissism is on a continuum from mild, occasional, and subtle to the more ubiquitous, obvious or extreme behaviors of a Narcissistic Personality Disorder. Since narcissism is likely a part of everyone's ego wounded self, it is helpful to your personal growth and development to be aware of your level of narcissism.

Be honest with yourself - but not judgmental - regarding the presence and intensity of the following characteristics:

I generally take others' rejecting, critical, harsh, shut-down, or diminishing behaviour personally. I tell myself that when others choose to behave in uncaring ways toward me, it is my fault - it is about me not being good enough or me doing something wrong. I make others' choices - to be open or closed, loving or unloving - about me.

I frequently judge and shame myself, trying to get myself to do things "right" so that I can have control over getting others' love, attention or approval. Getting others' love, attention and approval are vital to me.

I make others responsible for my worth, value, sense of aliveness and fullness. Others have to be kind, loving, approving of me, or sexually attracted to me, for me to feel that I'm okay. When others ignore me or are not attracted to me, I feel unworthy, depressed or empty inside.

I have a hard time having compassion for myself, so I expect others to have compassion for me when I feel anxious, depressed, angry, shamed or guilty, rather than taking responsibility for my feelings. If others lack compassion for me or criticize me, I turn things around onto them and blame them.

I lack empathy and compassion for the feelings of others, especially when I've behaved in ways that may be hurtful to others. I have a hard time recognizing or identifying with the feelings and needs of others.

When someone offers me valuable information about myself or 'tough love', I see it as an attack, rather than as a gift, and I generally attack back.

The DSM IV - The Diagnostic and Statistical Manual of Mental Disorders, states about people suffering from a Narcissistic Personality Disorder:

"Vulnerability in self-esteem makes individuals with Narcissistic Personality Disorder very sensitive to "injury" from criticism or defeat. Although they may not show it outwardly, criticism may haunt these individuals and may leave them feeling humiliated, degraded, hollow and empty. They may react with disdain, rage, or defiant counterattack. Such experience may lead to social withdrawal or an appearance of humility. Interpersonal relations are typically impaired due to problems derived from entitlement, the need for admiration, and the relative disregard for the sensitivities of others."

When in conflict with someone, or when someone behaves in a way I don't like, I often focus on getting them to deal with what they are doing, rather than focus on what I'm doing. I make them responsible for my choices and feelings, and I believe things will get better if I can get them to change.

I feel entitled to get what I want from others - whether it's money, sex, attention or approval. Others 'owe' me.

I often try to get away with things, such as not having to follow the rules or the law, and I'm indignant when I'm called to the carpet.

I see myself as special and entitled to do what I want, even if it's harmful to others.

I believe I should get credit for what I do and I should be recognized as superior, even if I do a mediocre job.

I am so unique and special that only other unique and special people can understand me. It is beneath me to associate with people who are not as special as I am. While some think I am arrogant, it is only because I'm truly so unique and special.

Because I'm so special, I have the right to demand what I want from others, and to manipulate others - with my charm, brilliance, anger or blame - into giving me what I want.

Again, all of us have some of these characteristics, and it is important to learn about them, rather than judge ourselves for them.

Narcissism can be healed. You can learn to define your worth, to give yourself the love and compassion you need to feel full inside, and to share love with others.

Healing from A Relationship With A Narcissist

Many of us have been there.

You met the person of your dreams - charming, intelligent, romantic, attentive, incredible chemistry and a great lover. You might have been told how wonderful you are, how this was the first time your lover had ever felt this way and had this level of connection, and you felt truly seen for the first time.

Perhaps there was a nagging unease that all this was happening too fast - that he or she couldn't possibly feel this way about you without knowing you better. But you were swept off your feet and finally decided to open your heart.

The confusion may have started then, as your lover pulled away and became critical. Or, it might have started after you married, and you found yourself with a partner different than the person you fell in love with.

Whether your relationship was two months or two years or two decades, it was likely tumultuous, confusing and painful. And if you were married and then divorced, it might have been more painful or even frightening.

There is much healing for you to do if you were in love with a narcissist.

The Process of Healing From Your Narcissistic Partner

1) First, you need to be very compassionate with yourself and let yourself grieve for the huge loss of what you had hoped for. It might seem easier to judge yourself for the big mistakes you believe you made, but self-judgment will keep you stuck. There is no possibility of healing when you judge yourself.

Each time the grief comes up, embrace it with kindness and caring toward yourself. Even though you know it's better to have ended this relationship; it's hard to let go of the intensity of a relationship with a narcissist. It's hard to imagine a future relationship that isn't boring compared to the intensity you've been experiencing.

2) Once some of the grief has subsided, then it's time to go inward and explore why you were vulnerable to this person. Was your partner giving you what you were not giving to yourself?

Was your partner seeing you and valuing you in the way you need to be seeing and valuing yourself? Did you ignore some red flags because you so wanted it all to be true?

Did you make excuses for your partner to avoid facing the truth? Did you give yourself up to try to have control over getting your partner to be loving to you again? What did you sacrifice to keep the relationship - your integrity, your financial security, your time with family and friends, your time for yourself, your inner knowing?

It's vitally important to be honest with yourself so that you don't end up feeling like a victim, and so that you have less of a chance of repeating this in a future relationship.

3) Educate yourself about narcissism. There are numerous books, websites and articles devoted to understanding narcissism. You can also buy my book on Narcissist. Since I'm certain that you don't want to repeat this, you need to do all you can to learn about what happened. You need to become sensitive to the numerous red flags so that you can pick them up very early in a subsequent relationship.

One of my clients shared that she had met a man six years ago, dated him a few times, and then they remained distant friends. Recently, when she was in his town, they saw each other, and she was very attracted to him. He came on strong, inviting her to join him on an upcoming European vacation. She felt uneasy, but a day later texted him to see if he wanted to have dinner with her. He never responded to the invitation. It took her only 24 hours to recognize these two red flags of narcissism - coming on strong and then disappearing. She was pleased that she found this out so soon! Instead of beating herself up for being attracted to another narcissist, she congratulated herself for staying open to the truth.

Since narcissists are often very attractive, any of us can become attracted. But whether or not we will pursue it depends on how much Inner Bonding work we have done.

Recovery from Narcissistic Abuse - To Get Your Life Back on Track

Narcissism or Narcissistic Personality Disorder (NPD) is a mental disorder that involves a persistent pattern of grandiosity. The person with this disorder constantly wants to be admired, is obsessed and infatuated with himself. The narcissistic individual also lacks compassion and empathy; is ruthless, egotistical, seeking dominance and gratification. To deal with and to live with a narcissistic can leave someone very traumatized due to the emotional abuse the narcissistic partner has caused. If you were married to a narcissist, you might find that it is difficult to escape from that relationship. If you do escape, your recovery will be long and painful. No matter how difficult the road to recovery is, you have to get through it so that your life will be back on track again.

• You have to know what the qualities of a narcissistic person are. It would include a frequent display of jealousy, infidelity, control, lying, and insecurity, verbal and even physical abuse. If these behaviours are not excused and are often tolerated, it would seem to the narcissistic person that they are acceptable. If you were successful in leaving a narcissistic partner or spouse, he would certainly lure you back again. As much as you love this person, you have to be firm in letting him know that his narcissistic behaviour may only be resolved with the help of a professional. He must seek professional assistance to correct his abusive personality, or he will not change. Being manipulated and believing that your ex will change on his own accord will only bring you back to a miserable and painful life.

• In recovering, you also need to realize that you are your complete person. When you decided to be in a relationship or marry a narcissistic person, you may have already developed a dependency on that person. He may have captured your heart with his attentive, generous and suave personality. This then resulted in your emotional dependency on him that eventually turned out as something for you to regret. Once escaped from the binding relationship with a narcissist, do your best to regain your emotional independence. It will help you to be firm and able to stand again on your own. Learn to love and accept your self-worth. Set your standards for whoever will soon come into your life. Do not accept anyone whose attributes are less than the standards you have set and you know you rightfully deserve.

• There are various materials that are now available online about dealing with narcissism. These resources will help you in understanding more about this disorder. Your gained knowledge will empower you and will make you realize what weaknesses have caused you to be captured in the narcissistic bait.

• You may also look for groups and organizations where you can be a part of. These groups offer help and an opportunity to communicate and interact with other people who have suffered and endured narcissistic relationships. These are the people whom you need to be with, together you can inspire one another and help one another obtain complete recovery and freedom from your experience.

Emotional Abuse - 8 Steps to Recovery

Do you remember the day your partner left you for someone new? That sick sinking feeling in your gut that you just weren't good enough? You tried so hard, and in the end, she was gone and with someone new.

At first, the silence was deafening, and you were so lonely, so very lonely. How could she be in love with you one day and love with someone else the next? You called. You texted. You just needed answers, but never got any response. You wanted a second chance to prove you could be better, but after a while, this passed, too, and you thought you were going to finally make it through the heartache.

You decide you don't want anything more to do with her and stop trying to contact her. BUT, now all those emotions are flooding back, and you just want to cry out in frustration after getting ANOTHER text, call or email from your ex. She hasn't heard from you in a while and misses you. She wants to get together, and so you do. She never really explains why she cheated or why she came back. She's just back, and you are on cloud nine... for a few months. Then the same thing happens again.

And here you are again, alone and still in love with the same person who "claimed" the breakup was your fault, that you weren't good enough. She's again ignoring your calls and texts wanting an explanation for why she walked out? The same person who was just posting all over Facebook about the "new" love in her life? And just like before, once you start to come out of the fog and start thinking it's over, all of a sudden, she wants you back? Do you feel trapped in a never-ending cycle of abuse, like a washing machine - rinse, spin, repeat, rinse, spin, repeat.

When you are together, does she make you feel like you are walking on eggshells, praying you don't do anything to upset her? Do you ignore or avoid calling her out on the hurtful things she says or does because you fear that every argument is your last? Does she constantly put you down and make you feel inferior to her? Have you stopped speaking to family and friends since you two have been together?

Wasn't this the same person who called you her soul mate? Do you remember she talked about her ex when you first got together? How crazy and jealous her ex was, and how glad she was to have found you. She told you that you were her soul mate.

Do you fall for her lies again, thinking you can recapture the early period of your relationship, when she was good and caring and kind? I don't like being the bearer of bad news, but I have to tell you, you're in relationship hell, stuck on a roller coaster, and to save yourself, you have to get away from this narcopath, who is nothing more than an emotional vampire.

Here's some hard-learned information. When you are desperately texting and calling to get "closure" by having your questions answered, you are feeding her energy. She thrives on this behaviour from you. It makes her feel powerful. She loves telling her new flame and all her friends how crazy psycho you are now. But, when you finally realize it's over, and stop calling and texting, guess what? She's not getting that supply of energy she is addicted to so much, and she thinks she's about to lose a great source of supply, so she starts calling and texting you. KNOW THIS: No normal person truly in love does this sort of thing. She is hovering - a term used to describe a narcopath who feels like you may be slipping away from her death grip.

It's imperative that you have no contact with this person. Even when she plays on your guilt or uses shame to trick you into "just talking to her", don't fall for it. Make yourself think like she thinks when you are dealing with her. She has no conscience or qualms about hurting you, so you take on the same attitude. It will continue, and the no contact may very well send her into a narcissistic rage. It doesn't matter what she does, stick to no contact.

In recovering from the emotional and verbal abuse of your former partner, here are eight steps you need to take to prepare yourself not to break the no contact rule:

1. Recognize that your love for this person is REAL. Ignoring this fact only sets you up for more abuse;

2. Recognize that this person lied to you, tricked you into falling in love. Think about it for a second. Had you met the person you are with now, would you have gone on a second date? Hell, no. It was an act, only an act. A narcopath is incapable of experiencing real emotion like love, empathy, compassion, guilt, etc. The only emotion I believe they feel is anger, and I'm sure you've seen the irrational rage common with narcopaths;

3. Accept the fact you will never get the answers to the burning questions you have;

4. Accept that the dream she promised was a lie;

5. Accept the fact that you can only change yourself, you cannot change her, and despite promises of change she always makes to get you to come back, she will not change;

6. Once you have internalized the first four steps, then you are ready to commit yourself to have absolutely no contact with her whatsoever. If you have children together, then limit the contact to ONLY discussions about the children;

7. Find a therapist to talk to. If you aren't comfortable talking to anyone face-to-face, then join a members-only site that offers advice and counselling; and finally

8. Find activities that help you restore your self-worth, your self-confidence and your joy. Colour therapy is an excellent activity for opening up your mind to new ideas and focusing on colouring puts you in a positive state of mind. EBT is good if you understand how it's done.

Best Tips to Recover from Narcissistic Abuse

How to heal from emotional abuse starts by recognizing that you have a problem. Even if you have already severed ties from an abusive relationship, it doesn't mean that everything will just go back to being alright.

There is an invisible energy stream that still exists between you and your previous abusive partner. It prevents you from being able to move forward with your life as you still unconsciously carry the emotional burden caused by the narcissist. You need to actively work from separating yourself in mind and soul to be able to break free from it. You will soon learn how as you continue to read along.

It is very helpful to regard yourself as a survivor and a winner instead of a victim. It immediately empowers you and gives you back control of your life. Here are some tips on how to heal from emotional abuse:

Understand that it's not your fault

Once you can find comfort in the fact that it's not your fault, you will begin to realize that you are not the cause of negative experiences you have gone through as opposed to what your abuser made you believe.

Confide in a close friend or relative

The people you trust will be able to provide you with the love and support at this critical time of healing. Talking about what you have gone through will help you better understand and accept your experience of abuse.

Discover coping tools

Find out what helps you express your emotions, release anger or grief. Writing in a journal, composing poems or songs, painting, any sport or playing a musical instrument can help you cope and let out your feelings. It will aid you in taking your mind off the pain you suffered and replace it with good and happy memories.

Take care of yourself

Learn to look after yourself first before taking care of others. Believe that you are worthy of respect, love and acceptance just like everybody else. Take pride in your unique qualities and improve on your weaknesses. You have to have faith in yourself first before other people do

CHAPTER 6

OVERCOMING AND RECOVERING FROM CODEPENDENCY

Shedding Codependency - 3 Tips for Overcoming Codependent Tendencies

Codependency is a term that has been used primarily to describe some of the common characteristics and behaviors that occur in people who are closely involved with an addict. These traits, which include excessive levels of tolerance for damaging behavior from their addicted loved one, a tendency to try to "rescue" or save the addict from his or her behavior, extreme caretaking tendencies, and a sense of responsibility for the addict's choices can all fall under the heading of codependency. These same traits can be found in other relationship dynamics where one person is behaving in destructive ways, such as in abusive scenarios. Here is three tips for overcoming codependent tendencies:

1. Consider it a act of love to allow the person you are protecting, defending, or making excuses for to face responsibility for his or her actions. The fact is, by trying to control his or her behavior, by shielding him or her from consequences, you become part of the system that allows these behaviors to continue. Without consequences, your loved one has no motive to change.

2. Begin to take better care of yourself. Make a conscious effort to shift focus away from solving your partner's problems, and consider your own needs in terms of diet, vitamins and supplements, and exercise. Eat healthy, unprocessed, organic foods whenever possible. Take vitamins and supplements according to your naturopath or other health practitioner's recommendations. Fish oil and a food-based multivitamin are a good start for many people. Exercise according to your doctor's recommendations, ideally doing 45 minutes of cardiovascular exercise 5 times a week. These activities not only focus on you and improve health, but send your mind the message that you are worth the effort and care.

3. Begin imagining your own life, your own dreams and aspirations, and spend regular time focused on that rather than focusing on what your loved one is doing. Allowing yourself to spend some time daydreaming and fantasizing about your ideal future in detail - how it will look, sounds, taste, feel, and smell - will increase your motivation and likelihood of seeing it manifest in reality.

Overcome Codependency - Discover the Freedom of Emotional Independence

Codependency has been defined in many different ways. Originally, it referred to the dynamic which is created when the support person of an alcoholic/addict becomes attached to being needed by that person and begins to unconsciously (or consciously) enable their destructive behavior, thereby maintaining the alcoholic's/addict's debilitation. Since then, codependency has begun to be defined more broadly. In order to fully understand what it means to be codependent, let's first define what it means to be emotionally independent.

Emotional independence is the ability to consistently meet your own needs. It means knowing how to pay attention to yourself, validate yourself, and provide yourself with a sense of self-worth. It is about fulfilling your own emotional needs rather than going outside yourself to have those needs met by other people. No one lives in a vacuum, so of course you are bound to receive attention, validation, etc. from the people you interact with, however, there is a vital distinction between receiving those gifts and being dependent upon them. Is having someone compliment you the icing on your cake, or is it your whole cake? Do you enjoy getting attention from the people you care about or do you need that attention to feel good about yourself?

Looking at emotional independence in this way, it becomes clear that emotional dependence, or codependency, does not exist as a specific label, but as a spectrum of interrelatedness. Therefore, codependency is herein defined as the degree to which you are reliant upon other people to meet your emotional needs. As you go along with book, consider what percentage of your emotional wellbeing you take care of in-house and what percentage you outsource. Is this a balance which is serving you or a lopsided arrangement which leaves you feeling needy and insatiable?

Changing yourself...

A vicious cycle:

The need for other people's recognition is a self-reinforcing cycle. Uncomfortable feelings arise (lonely, sad, empty, worthless, unlovable, etc.) and your first instinct is to do whatever is necessary to get rid of these "negative" emotions. Unable to supply yourself with the antidote to these feelings, you look to those around you to provide you with worth, fulfillment, love, or at least a distraction from the lack of those experiences. Each time you go outside yourself to get your emotional needs met, you are sending yourself some very strong messages.

Another people's attention is more valuable than mine. My own love is worthless. I am not capable of meeting my own needs. I will never feel whole on my own

These messages are internalized unconsciously and reinforce both the "negative" feelings you were experiencing originally, and the belief that you are dependent upon other people's attention/approval/validation, etc. The reliance upon other people's validation increases as the value you place on your own recognition plummets.

Breaking the cycle:

Breaking this cycle begins with becoming aware of your emotions.

When you have the urge to reach out to someone for emotional support, resist the temptation to react to that urge. Instead, turn your focus inward. What feelings are is you experiencing? What do you want to avoid by going outside yourself? Is what emotions does being alone bring up for you (lonely, afraid, bored, anxious, etc.)? Just sit with those feelings and try to allow them without judgment.

Notice the subtle reward of paying attention to yourself. Self-recognition is a much quieter experience than being recognized by others. It may be difficult to detect it's presence at first but look for it. You are breaking a habit, changing yourself, becoming more self-reliant. That is something to be proud of. Can you get in touch with that feeling?

Get in the practice of stopping and paying attention to yourself whenever you feel needy. Even if you later decide to seek out attention from someone else, you have taken the time to pay attention to yourself first. You has valued your own recognition. You are learning to validate yourself internally.

Changing your relationships...

We tend to be drawn to people who have a similar degree of emotional dependence to our own. If you rated yourself on the extreme end of the codependency spectrum, chances are, you have several people in your life who are in the same range. The "co" in codependency refers to the mutual emotional dependence people develop with one another. Both parties have become accustomed to needing to be needed so when one person begins to be less needy, this can disrupt the relationship.

Set and maintain boundaries. This isn't just about learning to say "no" to doing people favors. It can also mean declining invitations, choosing to keep some aspects of yourself private, making unpopular choices, protecting yourself from the judgment or verbal abuse of others, etc. It is about valuing and asserting your own interests. This is not selfish, it is self-loving. It is not about saying "no" to others, it is about saying "yes" to yourself and honouring your needs.

When you create a boundary with someone, notice the sense of self-respect this brings. If you are not used to putting yourself first, you may also have feelings of guilt, shame, or self-judgment arise. See if you can dig beneath those feelings to the satisfaction of having taken care of yourself.

Cultivate an interest in yourself. Discover ways of connecting with you. Exploring a hobby, you have always wanted to pursue, taking a class you are interested in, journaling your thoughts and emotions, writing poetry or doing something creative, taking walks, photography, anything that you find fulfilling. You are learning new ways of bringing yourself a sense of worth and joy.

Prioritize your new, self-worth building activities. If a friend invites you to lunch but you had already been planning to go to your yoga class, it may be tempting to drop everything to enjoy your friend's company. The problem is, that sends those same destructive messages ("Other people's attention is more valuable than mine. Spending time with someone else is more fulfilling than pursuing my own interests. Spending time with someone else is more appealing than spending time with me"). Make your commitment to your new activities sacred. It is a promise you are making to yourself. Imagine what kind of a message you are sending yourself each time you keep that promise.

Codependency is a difficult habit to break, but it can be done. Emotional independence is freedom in the purest sense. You are a whole, fulfilled, joyful person all on your own. Since your mood and wellbeing are no longer dependent upon others, there is no need to manipulate, to pull on people for validation. You can be fully present and authentic. Emotional independence is a challenging path to follow, but the empowerment, freedom, and self-respect you will find on this journey will sustain and motivate you along the way.

Three Ways to Overcome Codependent Relationships

Of all relationships, codependent relationships are probably the least healthy ones. If you happen to be in one of these relationships, you should quickly figure out how to solve the issue of codependency or simply call it quits. Whether you are codependent or she is, if the problem is left unsolved, it's going to have negative consequences on you and her in the future. Below is three ways to overcome codependent relationships.

Therapy/Counseling

If you have the financial means, this is probably the best solution. Having professional help is the fastest and most effective way to finding out why has your relationship become codependent and what needs to be done for you and her to go back to those wonderful times you had at the beginning of the relationship. It is also important to note that professional help is unbiased compared to a relative or close friend. A more familiar person will think of what's best for you not for the couple while the professional will consider both parties' interest in the issue at hand.

Let Your Partner Know What's Wrong

Everyone has needs and those needs need to be satisfied. At some point not expressing your needs or feelings will lead to a bigger need of attention which will eventually lead to selfishness. Selfishness is one of the main symptoms in codependent relationships. One of the partners feels the other one should drive all their attention towards them which is not healthy for both partners. Talking about it is the easiest way out of it so don't hesitate to communicate your needs to your partner. After all, if she wasn't interested in making you happy then you need to ask yourself why she's with you.

Participate in Different Activities

This may sound controversial but believe it or not, some activities are better done alone. Usually things are better done in pairs but if it's making you and your partner uncomfortable it's time to switch it up a little. For example, training sessions, girls night out, boys night out, basically any activity you would do better without your partner around. Why? It'll give you the opportunity to meet new people and sometimes it's all it takes to make you or her realize how dependent you've become and how you or her need to change.

When it comes to relationships, drama is inevitable. You can't predict when something will go wrong in the beginning because you seem to be in heaven. However, if you end up in one of that bad relationship, there are very few options for you to choose. Should you try and resolve the issue or move on? One thing's for sure, if it's one of those codependent relationships, you may want to opt for a solution as soon as possible since it can only get worse from this point on.

Recovering from Codependency

Codependency underlies all addictions. The core symptom of "dependency" manifests as reliance on a person, substance, or process (i.e., activity, such as gambling or sex addiction). Instead of having a healthy relationship with yourself, you make something or someone else more important. Over time, your thoughts, feelings, and actions revolve around that other person, activity, or substance, and you increasingly abandon your relationship with yourself.

Recovery entails a 180-degree reversal of this pattern to reconnect with, honour, and act from your core self. Healing develops the following characteristics:

* You're authentic

* You're autonomous

* You're capable of intimacy

* Your values, thoughts, feelings, and actions become integrated and congruent

Change is not easy. It takes time and involves the following four steps:

1. Abstinence

Abstinence or sobriety is necessary to recover from codependency. The goal is to bring your attention back to yourself, to have an internal, rather than external, "locus of control." This means that your actions are primarily motivated by your values, needs, and feelings, not someone else's. You learn to meet those needs in healthy ways. Perfect abstinence or sobriety isn't necessary for progress, and it's impossible concerning codependency with people. You need and depend upon others and therefore give and compromise in relationships. Instead of abstinence, you learn to detach and not control, people-please, or obsess about others. You become more self-directed and autonomous.

If you're involved with an abuser or addict or grew up as the child of one, you may be afraid to displease your partner, and it can require great courage to break that pattern of conceding our power to someone else.

2. Awareness

It's said that denial is the hallmark of addiction. This is true whether you're an alcoholic or in love with one. Not only do codependents deny their addiction - whether to a drug, activity, or a person - they deny their feelings, and especially their needs, particularly emotional needs for nurturing and real intimacy.

You may have grown up in a family where you weren't nurtured, your opinions and feelings weren't respected, and your emotional needs weren't adequately met. Over time, rather than risk rejection or criticism, you learned to ignore your needs and feelings, believed that you be wrong. Some decided to become self-sufficient and find comfort in sex, food, drugs, or work.

All of this leads to low self-esteem. To reverse these destructive habits, you first must become aware of them. The most damaging obstacle to self-esteem is negative self-talk. Most people aren't aware of the internal voices that push and criticize them - their "Pusher," "Perfectionist," and "Critic."

3. Acceptance

Healing essentially involves self-acceptance. This is not only a step but a life-long journey. People come to therapy to change themselves, not realizing that the work is about accepting themselves. Ironically, before you can change, you have to accept the situation. As they say, "What you resist, persists."

In recovery, more about yourself is revealed that requires acceptance, and life itself presents limitations and losses to accept. This is maturity. Accepting reality opens the doors of possibility. Change then happens. New ideas and energy emerge that previously were stagnated from self-blame and fighting reality. For example, when you feel sad, lonely, or guilty, instead of making yourself feel worse, you have self-compassion, soothe yourself, and take steps to feel better.

Self-acceptance means that you don't have to please everyone for fear that they won't like you. You honour your needs and unpleasant feelings and are forgiving of yourself and others. This good-will toward yourself allows you to be self-reflective, without being self-critical. Your self-esteem and confidence grow, and consequently, you don't allow others to abuse you or tell you what to do. Instead of manipulating, you become more authentic and assertive and are capable of greater intimacy.

4. Action

Insight without action only gets you so far. To grow, self-awareness and self-acceptance must be accompanied by new behaviour. This involves taking risks and venturing outside your comfort one. It may involve speaking up, trying something new, going somewhere alone, or setting a boundary. It also means setting internal boundaries by keeping commitments to yourself or saying "no" to your Critic or other old habits you want to change. Instead of expecting others to meet all your needs and make you happy, you learn to take actions to meet them and do things that give you fulfilment and satisfaction in your life.

Each time you try out new behaviour or take a risk, you learn something new about yourself and your feelings and needs. You're creating a stronger sense of yourself, as well as self-confidence and self-esteem. This builds upon itself in a positive feedback loop vs the downward spiral of codependency, which creates more fear, depression, and low self-esteem.

Healing Codependency

Healing codependency does not mean curing codependency. Healing codependency is a process. Healing always begins by recognizing the problem. Knowledge is power, and that is true when we talk about Healing Codependency.

Let us continue the journey of understanding the process of Healing Codependency. Ask yourself these questions: Am I codependent? What does this mean? What codependent behaviours do I have? What does it cost me? These are essential questions as one begins the journey of healing and questions that need to be explored. I suggest you begin a journal and start recording your responses to these questions, allowing it to be your touchstone.

In addition to the journal, a group setting in the form of support groups facilitates the healing process. The community you live in may have some Codependency Support Groups. If not, perhaps try to find the name of a psychotherapist who specializes in addictions and understands codependency. I have found Al-Anon groups to be effective if there is not a Codependency Support Group.

Developing an understanding of the roots of your codependency can provide a foundation for your healing. Many codependents are adult children of alcoholics/addicts and come from dysfunctional families. The journey of healing is about the family of origin work as you discover the role and, the rules you were given and general dynamics from your first family. Most adult children from dysfunctional families remain in those roles, abide by those rules and, struggle with dynamics that are similar to those learned in their family of origins, repeating patterns with their significant other and their children today. However, please keep in mind that as wonderful as insight can be, insight alone will not heal your pain nor provide you with the healing necessary for changing codependent behaviours and patterns.

Learning emotional detachment will assist you in early recovery and be a mainstay throughout your recovery program. Detaching is about learning to balance self in relationship with others. It is the beginning of boundary work, which you will hear much about at support groups and in your recommended readings. Detaching allows your emotional reactivity to lower and an emotional space to open, creating the opportunity for less dependency in relationships. It will be in this new space that one can begin to develop a sense of "who am I?" Needs wants, and feelings can begin to be identified and communicated as you move toward less codependent relationships.

Communication skills, self-esteem building and improving how you manage stress will also be areas that will need to be addressed in your codependency recovery. These "tools" will assist in regaining one's sense of self that was lost in codependent relationships. Recovery is about regaining your power that was lost in the dynamics of codependent relationships. It is about feeling empowered to live one's life without the need of approval, the fear of abandonment, of being preoccupied with pleasing others, about caring too much, and in general over functioning in relationships. Recovery is claiming back self.

www.ingramcontent.com/pod-product-compliance
Lightning Source LLC
Chambersburg PA
CBHW070859080526
44589CB00013B/1131